MYRES SMITH McDOUGAL

Appreciations of an Extraordinary Man

D1256659

MYRES SMITH McDOUGAL

Appreciations of an Extraordinary Man

Yale Law School · New Haven, Connecticut

On the cover: Myres Smith McDougal's office at Yale Law School, 1993.
Photograph by Jim Dow.

On May 7, 1998, when Myres Smith McDougal died at the age of ninety-one, the world lost a formidable legal mind, a stunningly prolific author, and a great human being. The Yale Law School community lost an inspiring teacher, a respected colleague, and, for many, a lifelong friend and mentor.

In the following pages are gathered the thoughts and remembrances of many of Mac's friends and colleagues. Together, they honor and celebrate the remarkable life of this extraordinary man.

Anthony T. Kronman
Dean, Yale Law School

New Haven, August, 1999

CONTENTS

:

SPEECHES

Delivered at the Memorial
October 4, 1998

ANTHONY T. KRONMAN
Dean, Yale Law School

THE CENTER OF THE CIRCLE

I want to welcome you to this afternoon of remembrances celebrating the extraordinary life of our friend and teacher Myres McDougal. The number of people who have gathered here—and even more, the distance that many of you have traveled—speaks volumes about the breadth of Mac's circle of friends, a circle that literally encompasses the globe. Mac stood at the center of a web of allegiances and scholarly collaborations that stretched from New Haven to Tokyo to Bangkok to Delhi to Frankfurt to London and back to New Haven again. During my deanship, I have done a fair bit of traveling, and wherever I go I am always asked two questions: How is the School doing? And how is my friend Mac? I now know that Mac has friends in every great city on earth, and you who are here today are the representatives of that larger assembly.

The life at the center of this global web of friendships had its own center in work. Mac had a gigantic passion for work. He derived visible pleasure from it and managed as effectively as anyone who has ever taught at the School to convey his excitement and enthusiasm for work to the students who were lucky enough to study with him. Not too long before Mac died, he was in and out of the hospital several times. His long-time assistant and dear friend Cheryl DeFilippo would accompany Mac to the hospital and then back again to Evergreen Woods. I spoke with Cheryl after one of these hospital stays—six weeks before Mac's death—and asked how he was doing. She said, "Well, Mac is physically weak but his spirits are strong. When they told him he was about to be released from the hospital, he said that was good news because he had a great deal of work to do and needed to get back to it." The gospelist John wrote, "Let us work, for soon it will be night and then no work can be done." No one understood that sentiment more profoundly than Myres McDougal.

Yet Mac's passion for his work and the work itself—the magnificence of all those books on the library shelf—does not by itself explain why so many have made the trip to be here in New Haven today. As great and brilliant a teacher and scholar as Mac was, he was also a remarkable human being. This is something that everyone who came into his radiant circle understood and grew to appreciate.

In the months since Mac's death, I have received countless letters from former students and friends around the world, and they all have one characteristic in common. Each of these letters expresses immense admiration and respect for Mac's intellectual achievements, but each then goes on to recount an incident of one kind or another that touched the writer in a personal way. I could spend the rest of the afternoon sharing with you the anecdotes recounted in these letters. Let me share just a few.

When Winston Nagan arrived in New Haven in 1975, he had heard a fair bit about Mac and Mac's jurisprudence. He was eager to meet the great man and enrolled in Mac's international law class. Winston describes his experience as follows:

When I came to Yale, I signed up for Mac's class on international law. I had not yet settled on an advisor or what program I was going to do. In the first class Mac was doing everything possible to get a rise out of his students. Near the end of class, he stated a proposition about the prospects for peace in the Middle East that was clearly not tenable for anyone who had actually visited the region as I had done quite recently. To break the silence I challenged him and we went back and forth. At the end of the class, without any display of emotion he said, "I'd like to see Mr. Nagan in my office." All the Yalies came over to me and said, "He's going to throw you out of the Law School. How could you challenge him like that? He's a famous authority." Having thus been reminded of my tenuous status at Yale, I trundled up to Mac's office. As I entered the office I saw a little sign that said *"illegitimati non carborundum,"* which roughly translated means "don't let the bastards grind you down." I thought, "I hope he doesn't think I am a bastard with any capacity to grind him down." I sat down, noticing the broad smile on his face. He said, "Who is your advisor?" I responded, "I'd hoped you would be my advisor." "You've got me," Mac replied.

Sophie Tierong Zhu today lives in Changsha, China. After Mac's death, she wrote a beautiful letter recalling her time here in New Haven in the late 1940s with her husband Ifan, who was a J.S.D. student at the time and was later driven to suicide during the cultural revolution when he stood up for the idea that government means the rule of law, not men—an idea that Sophie says Ifan always associated with his great teacher Myres McDougal. In her letter, Sophie describes the evenings she and Ifan spent at the McDougal home with Mac's young son John playing with his electric trains and operating a home movie camera. She remembers her time in New Haven as being lit up with Mac's warmth and welcome. "Mac made us feel at home," Sophie writes, "and gave the Graduate Program life."

Then there is the letter I received recently from Cecil Olmstead who, in addition to remarking on Mac's greatness as an intellect, goes on to say that he and Mac shared more than a common passion for ideas. They also shared an upbringing in the rural South and Cecil recounts the many long hours he and Mac spent reminiscing about fishing in cool streams and listening to great Southern politicians like Bilbow and others on the stump in their small home towns.

Each of these letters remarks on Mac's remarkable courtesy—his *Southern* courtesy, as it is characterized over and over again. In this increasingly barbaric age Mac's courtesy was indeed a rarity and pleasure. It was refreshing. But Mac's humanity went well beyond being well-mannered and polite in the superficial sense. Mac had a talent for friendship that very few people possess. He was a virtuoso of friendship. He was able almost instantly to take a deep interest in the young person who had just stepped into his office for the first time, and to put himself at the center of that person's life. Within minutes, a friendship had formed, and when Mac made a friend, the friendship lasted forever. Mac's friendships were not relations of a day or a week or a year. They endured for a lifetime, and if you were Mac's friend, he would follow you wherever you went. These weren't passive friendships, either. They were very active friendships. Mac sought at every turn to be of help to his friends and to do whatever was within his power to assist them in their careers—and I might add that it was often within Mac's power to do quite a bit.

I might also add that Mac's famous capacity for friendship never to my knowledge compromised his formidable critical powers or deterred him from speaking with anything less than perfect bluntness, if the occasion required. I remember many lunches with Mac in the Faculty Dining Room. Mac would come in with a hearty laugh, join the table discussion, and ask what we were talking about. He would listen quietly for a minute or two, and then would turn to some learned colleague who had just made a very large statement of some sort and say, "that's the most damn ridiculous thing I've ever heard in my life." At that point you knew that lunch had begun.

Mac's good manners, as I say, never caused him to conceal his true views. One 1970 graduate of the Law School—a man named Rob Brown who now practices law in Rochester—wrote some years ago in his Class Notes for the *Yale Law Report* that his most vivid memory from law school was of a paper he wrote for Mac's course on Law, Science, and Policy. "I worked hard on it," Rob said, "But I didn't think I had done a terribly good job. I turned it in and much to my surprise it got a very high mark with a note at the bottom of the page that said, 'A fine job, Mr. Brown. I didn't think you had it in you.'"

This might seem like a paradox: the well-mannered Southern gentleman who is also an uncompromising man of science. But it isn't really a paradox at all. Good manners for Mac meant treating you with respect, and treating you with respect meant drawing you into the conversation, into the inquiry, into the search for truth. Mac was a tremendous friend, but friendship is in all its forms a kind of sharing. What Mac wanted most of all was to share his own intellectual vitality and passion for his work with his friends, and he knew that the very best way of doing this is always to speak honestly and to keep the truth in view.

I have been talking about Mac the man. I'd like now to say a word or two about his work. Others can speak at greater length about Mac's scholarship; they know it far better than I do. But I would like to make two basic points about Mac's intellectual achievement.

First, the formidable architecture of Mac's jurisprudence and the imposing vocabulary which goes with it has caused many to view his theory of law as something exotic, pursued by a few devoted students, but on the whole enjoying only a limited influence within the larger field of American academic legal studies. I think this view is deeply mistaken. Mac's policy science, as he called it, combines two basic ideas that are at the very core of legal studies in the United States today and which in fact define the reigning orthodoxy in American legal education. One is that the law is not a system of closed norms whose meaning is self-evident. A simple inspection of these norms shows that they do not contain within themselves an answer to the question of what ends they should be used to promote. We must begin our study of law, Mac argued, by acknowledging that law should be used for the advancement of shared goals and ideals, as an instrument of policy. Unless we put the law in this larger perspective, Mac said, we will never know how to ask, let alone to answer, the key questions that every legal theorist must address. Mac's other basic idea was that these questions of policy can themselves be approached in a rigorous and disciplined way—not in an ad hoc, slipshod fashion, moving from one question to the next without any guiding principles to structure the inquiry, but in a comprehensive and scientific manner. Mac was the first to formulate this ideal.

Second, I would emphasize the durability of Mac's guiding ideals, the ideals of democracy and dignity. These are the two words that carry the greatest moral weight in Mac's jurisprudential lexicon. In recent years, we have seen a measure of progress toward the realization of both ideals. The collapse of the Soviet Union and the surprising resurgence of democratic life in Eastern Europe and Latin America make the cause of democracy seem brighter today than it has ever been before. And the international human rights movement now has a vigor and influence it never possessed in the past. Our progress toward the ideals of democracy and dignity makes it easy to think their defense is a simple matter. What could be less debatable than the need to support democracy and dignity against their enemies? But this is an anachronistic view. It confuses the present with the past. We need to remember how difficult it has been, in the past, to stand up for these ideals in the way Mac did from the start. Mac was always clear about their importance, and he had the courage to say what needed to be said. No one on this faculty, indeed no law teacher in America, has done more in his lifetime to advance these two ideals. Mac did this through the great intellectual force of his writing. But he also did it through the example of his own commitment and the steady accumulation of a network of friends who themselves have contributed importantly to the advancement of democracy and dignity for people everywhere—a magnificent and lasting achievement.

Let me close by saying a word about Mac's relationship to the Yale Law School. When I became dean, I said that it was my ambition to broaden the horizons of the Yale Law School and to make it a school for the whole world. I said that the Yale Law School had become a great national institution, but that it needed now to look beyond our national borders, to take students from every corner of the world and to take an interest in the legal problems of their countries. Every law school dean in America today has the word "globalization" on his or her lips. I am no longer sure I know what this word means, but it has certainly become a fashionable term. Long before it was fashionable, however—long before it was even a term—Mac understood what globalization meant, and everything I have accomplished in the way of giving the program here at the Yale Law School a more global perspective builds on Mac's great accomplishments and would have been absolutely impossible without them. The legacy of internationalism that Mac bequeathed to the Yale Law School is one of his greatest and most enduring gifts to the School.

I have sometimes wondered what so fascinated Mac about the great empty spaces of the world—Antarctica, the floor of the sea, outer space. The Law School's portrait of Mac shows him holding a copy of his great treatise on the law of outer space. What drew Mac to these empty places? In one sense the answer is obvious. These are the places that have not yet been inscribed by the law. These are the empty places that John Locke called the state of nature (by which he mainly meant North America). Here, all the foundational questions of law remain to be addressed. A great mind, looking for some elbow room, will inevitably be drawn to these places.

But there is another empty place to which Mac was drawn. The emptiest place of all is the future. It is that great blank sheet on which every scholar wants to inscribe his own thoughts so that, as Justice Holmes remarked, unborn listeners can hear the music of the scholar's ideas and dance to them long after their maker is gone. Mac understood the passion Holmes describes. He wrote for the ages. He planted more than a few flags in the country of the future, and I assure you that in years to come we will see his claim to that kingdom expand.

ANDREW R. WILLARD

Associate Research Scholar, Yale Law School
President, The Policy Sciences Center, Inc. and the Society for the Policy Sciences

A LIFE OF AND ABOUT HUMAN DIGNITY

Myres Smith McDougal, founder of the Policy-Oriented School of Jurisprudence, was the eldest of three sons born to Lula Bell (Smith) and Luther Love McDougal. He was born on November 23, 1906, in the farming community of Burton, in the hill country of northern Mississippi. His brother, Luther, was close to three years younger than he and the youngest of the three boys, Bolivar Smith, known simply as Smith, was seven years younger than Myres. Although he had contact with many of his relatives, Myres and his parents and brothers spent a great deal of time with his maternal grandparents at their farm in New Hope. It was here that young Myres learned to hunt and fish and farm. His grandfather even made a miniature plough for him to use. It was also in this extended family context where Myres began to understand the importance of stable relationships and the power of human agency. His keen sense of family and identity and of interpersonal dynamics and of place was developed here as well. It was his maternal grandmother who impressed on him that he was not only a Mississippian and a native of the United States, but a member of the world.

When Myres was roughly of school age, his parents settled in Booneville, a fifteen-mile journey from New Hope. His father's medical practice had grown and stabilized, and Booneville was picked, presumably, for its central location. Myres attended public school in Booneville and was a leading student. He delivered his high school graduation valedictory speech on the subject of thrift. It was also in high school where Myres was introduced to the study of international law.

Of course, life was not all studies. As the oldest son, Myres was given responsibility for taking care of the family cows. He enjoyed this work, and it may have helped to shape his future success as a contestant in livestock judging contests. Myres also participated in some of childhood's more mischievous activities. He and his best friend, Glenn Bolton, were skilled with slingshots and apparently caused no small amount of trouble for local bullies. Mac recalled once when the two of them held off the whole town from the barn overlooking the railroad.

A major event in Myres' life occurred when he was twelve. He came down with acute nephritis. His father gathered the best doctors in town around his bed and they agreed that there was nothing to be done. His father would not accept this, and Mac remembered his father saying, "This is not going to be." He took young Myres to Hot Springs, Arkansas and after three weeks of bathing in the hot springs, the illness subsided and the two of them returned to Booneville. Another constitutive event in Myres' early years took place when he was fifteen or so. He would spend much of each summer on his parents' and grandparents' farms, working on various activities. On this particular afternoon, the foreman of his parents' farm was teasing Myres, as was his style. However, for reasons that Mac could not recall, he decided that he had had enough and challenged the man. To everyone's surprise, Mac won the fight. On more than one occasion, Mac explained how important this event was in building his confidence and respect.

In 1922, Myres enrolled at the University of Mississippi in Oxford. He had an uncle living in Oxford, so he had visited many times before starting school. His years at Ole Miss were filled with hard work and play. I suspect that it was during his college years that he began to refer to himself as Mac. To his family and extended family, he was and always would be known as Myres. (Although Mac never knew why, he was named "Myres" for one of his father's favorite teachers in medical school in Louisville, Kentucky.)

In college, Mac excelled in classics, and by his senior year was teaching Latin and Greek. He also became the editor of the school newspaper, *The Mississippian*. The highlight of his tenure as editor was his defense of the university chancellor's decision to permit the teaching of evolutionary theory. Mac wrote the article defending the chancellor and distributed copies of it in Jackson, the state capitol. Later, the chancellor would reciprocate by supporting Mac in his application for a Rhodes Scholarship. In 1927, at the age of twenty, Mac graduated from the University of Mississippi with a B.A. and an M.A. and later received his LL.B. He had won the Rhodes Scholarship and was on his way to England.

Mac spent three wonderful years at Oxford. He had a spacious and beautiful suite at St. John's College and the good fortune to have Sir William Holdsworth, the great legal historian, as his tutor. This was not the case at first. Apparently there was a new tutor in law at St. John's to whom Mac had been assigned. Mac was unimpressed with his knowledge of law and refused to see him. This caused a bit of a stir and Holdsworth intervened, offering to become Mac's tutor. Holdsworth was quite influential in teaching, mentoring, and, in some measure, serving as a father figure to Mac. It was Holdsworth who supported Mac's desire to become a scholar and directed him to Yale.

Holdsworth was not the only important scholar and teacher in Mac's Oxford experience. Mac attended James L. Brierly's lectures on international law and took down in longhand the text to the original edition of *The Law of Nations*. Brierly, like Holdsworth, invited Mac to his home on a regular basis. This personal style suited Mac, and, as is well known, Mac developed and practiced such a style with generations of his own students. The culminating event in Mac's Oxford experience was his performance on his exams. He achieved "double firsts," rare even for an Englishman, let alone for an American. Of all of his life's achievements, this was the one of which Mac was most proud.

After receiving his B.A. and B.C.L., Mac returned to the United States. He entertained the idea of working at a New York law firm, and contacted four firms. He received four offers but decided instead to pursue his interest in legal scholarship at Yale. When Mac arrived in New Haven, it was a thriving northern industrial city. Elm trees grew everywhere and trolleys were available for long rides out to Spring Glen on Whitney Avenue or to Westville on Whalley Avenue. Riding stables were in East Rock Park. It was also the time of the Great Depression and Mac remembered seeing men in suits trying to sell apples on York Street. At Yale, the new Sterling Law Building and the Payne Whitney Gymnasium would soon open.

The new approach to the study of law known as American Legal Realism was flowering at Yale when Mac arrived. At first, Mac was antagonistic toward this approach to law, for it challenged head-on the understanding of law he had cultivated in England. However, after about six months of fighting with Yale Law Professor Wesley Sturges, Mac finally woke up one day and admitted to himself, "the son of a bitch is right." In class that day, when Sturges called on him, Mac shocked him with his response. From that day on, Mac's sense of himself was that he was a committed member of the Realist school. When Mac graduated in 1931 with his J.S.D., Dean Charles Clark told him that he was going to "farm" him out to the University of Illinois Law School in Urbana. If, after a few years, Mac had proved that he was truly a Realist, Clark would invite him back to be on the Yale faculty.

It was during his year at Yale as a graduate student that Mac met his future wife, Frances Lee. She was a graduate student in economics at Yale, and the two of them met at a dance at the YMCA in New Haven. She was a member of the Lee family of Virginia, which put her in a special class for a southerner like Mac. They were married in Washington, D.C., on December 27, 1933. They had one son, John Lee McDougal, who was born in 1940.

Mac enjoyed Urbana, and when the invitation to return to Yale came from Dean Clark, he hesitated before accepting. He also had accepted a visiting post at the University of Chicago Law School, so he arranged to be in Chicago in 1935 even though his appointment at Yale began in 1934. It was during this brief stay in Chicago that Mac met Harold Lasswell. Mac had read in *The New York Times* a review of Lasswell's new book, *World Politics and Personal Insecurity*. The reviewer had concluded that it was a great book and that there would be people who would understand it even if he did not. When Mac had finished teaching his course one morning after reading the review, he noticed that Lasswell's name was on the door opposite the room where he had just finished teaching. Since there were noises still coming from this room, Mac decided to slip in and listen. Lasswell was applying psychoanalytic techniques to the auto-biography of H.G.Wells. At this time, Wells' autobiography was a Book of the Month Club selection and many people were reading it, including Mac. After listening to Lasswell, Mac felt that he could hear Wells tick. He never read another word of H.G.Wells after that morning. After the class, Mac introduced himself to Lasswell and thus began a lifelong friendship and collaboration that is unparalleled in the annals of higher education.

When Mac returned to Yale, he taught property law, though he also special-ized in what were called credit transactions and debtors estates. In the late 1930s, he was asked to teach a course on jurisprudence, and he used this oppor-tunity to invite Lasswell, who was in New York, to teach the course with him. They called the course "Property in a Crisis Society," and over the years it was transformed into the familiar course on "Law, Science and Policy."

During World War II, Mac commuted between Washington and New Haven. He was assistant general counsel in the Lend-Lease Administration and gen-eral counsel in the Office of Foreign Relief and Rehabilitation Operations. In both contexts, Mac learned how to operate effectively in a hierarchical organi-zation. Although there was less time for scholarship, it was during the war that Mac wrote with Lasswell their most well-known article, "Legal Education and Public Policy: Professional Training in the Public Interest." The article, which was written in the Blackstone Hotel in Washington, was and still is a call to transform legal education so that all who practice law would be better equipped to carry out their tasks as servants and statesmen of the public interest.

After the war, Lasswell joined Mac as a permanent member of the Yale Law School faculty and they began in earnest their project, which became an enter-prise to transform legal education. One of the primary vehicles for carrying out this work was the Graduate Program at the Yale Law School. Mac ran this program for students from all over the world for twenty-five years. Like his teachers at Oxford, Mac always took an interest in his students' entire lives. He was interested in helping them to develop not only their intellectual capability but also their ability to achieve their goals in reference to any value, from power and wealth to affection and rectitude. This is not to say that Mac did not teach and promote his conception of law, which included the tasks that teachers, lawyers, and other decisionmakers must carry out in order to perform adequately the varied roles they play. Mac felt strongly that the intellectual procedures he recommended could be used individually for greater self realization as well as collectively to further the cause of human dignity.

In addition to building and guiding the Graduate Program, Mac turned his attention back to international law after the close of World War II. There were many reasons for this change in his focus of attention. The experience of the war itself and of the newly perceived responsibility facing the United States were among the conditioning factors. Lasswell also encouraged him to turn in this direction. As a result, it was in the field of international law that Mac developed his general approach to law. To this day, many people do not realize that Mac's jurisprudence is a theory of and about all law in all contexts and is in no way limited to being only a jurisprudence for international law.

During the late 1940s and early 1950s, Mac and Lasswell developed and refined their teaching materials for the "Law, Science and Policy" seminar. They also began teaching a course called "The World Community and Law: A Contemporary International Law," which developed subsequently into "The Public Order of the World Community." Although Mac wrote and published a great deal in the ten years following his return to Yale, it wasn't until after his eye trouble began in 1955 that he embarked on the sustained and focused research and publication program for which he became so well known. Detailed and comprehensive demonstrations of the jurisprudence he was developing were published in reference to the international law of war (1961), the international law of the sea (1962), the international law of outer space (1963), and the interpretation of international agreements (1967). Later, in 1980, his equally remarkable treatment of human rights was published. In 1992, the jurisprudence that Mac and Lasswell created was published in a two-volume work entitled, *Jurisprudence for a Free Society: Studies in Law, Science and Policy*.

Mac was not only a great scholar and teacher and friend. He was also active and effective in every organization in which he participated. These included professional associations and various forms of government service. He served as president of both the American Society of International Law and the Association of American Law Schools and was chairman of the board of The Policy Sciences Center. He was also a member of the *Institut de Droit International* and, as with his participation elsewhere, he was a stimulating presence in this specialized institution. Mac enjoyed controversy, and, regardless of venue, he would tackle every challenge with gusto. But his enthusiasm never undermined the quality of his work, which was characterized by its thoroughness, insight, and precision.

But the essential core of Mac's magnetism, what made him so special, was ultimately his character. He was at once a classic and brilliant scholar and a southern farm boy, and apt, sometimes hilarious sayings peppered his teaching and conversation. He was a big, handsome man, with a wonderfully infectious laugh, who was generous, warm, open, honest, and loyal. Perhaps it was Mac's utter authenticity that was so distinctive. He embraced "his People"—and this was a vast legion from all walks of life—and was loved in return. Quite simply, Mac put into daily practice his teaching of *and* about human dignity. He will be missed more than he ever could have imagined.

———

A good biography is no different than a good natural history. The author should be able to identify and track trends in the formation of the subject's character. Moreover, the factors that shaped or conditioned the trends need to be revealed and their interrelationships specified and understood. Hopefully, this very brief sketch provides a rough contour of the life of Myres Smith McDougal. But there is more to a biography of Mac than simply trends and conditions. A complete presentation would involve the clarification of his values, projections of possible futures for the jurisprudence he developed, and the detailed specification of alternatives for making more likely the eventuation of a future that is compatible with the public order of human dignity that Mac preferred.

W. MICHAEL REISMAN
Myres S. McDougal Professor of Law, Yale Law School

THEORY ABOUT LAW: JURISPRUDENCE FOR A FREE SOCIETY

Theory about law was the center of Myres McDougal's intellectual enterprise. Each of his treatises and monographs, even his occasional papers and court pleadings, every dissertation and, as many of you here know, the student papers done under his supervision were and had to be an explicit and intentional application of his theory. Whether it was resource use and planning in the Connecticut Valley, in the oceans or in outer space, whether it was the law of war or human rights, treaty interpretation or constitutional interpretation, each study tried to be an integrated application of the theory.

From the beginning, theory about law was McDougal's primary interest. Fresh from Oxford, a newly minted Analytical Positivist, he arrived at Yale and told a bemused Dean Clark that he intended to teach jurisprudence. And he did. Whether his course was negotiable instruments, debtors rights, property or any of the areas of international law he addressed, he was always teaching one year-long seminar on jurisprudence, closely analyzing the theories of others, while elaborating his own.

With the exception of the theory of the constitutive process, the jurisprudence was essentially completed in manuscript by the late 1950s. Many of you here today studied jurisprudence with McDougal from different versions of that manuscript, then called "Law, Science and Policy." For reasons biographers will explore, the manuscript was only published in 1992 in two volumes under the title of "Lasswell and McDougal, *Jurisprudence for a Free Society: Studies in Law, Science and Policy;*" a paperback student edition appeared in 1997. The dedication page of the volumes has three words: "To our students." To all of us here today.

Many modern theories of law trace their origins to a single insight. H.L.A. Hart saw that Austin's notion that law was the command of a political superior could not account for the authoritative component of law and addressed that missing item in the rest of his work. Hans Kelsen saw that historicist conceptions of law could not serve the needs of decision-makers in the modernizing multi-ethnic empire that was the Dual Monarchy and invented a "pure theory of law" to rise above them. McDougal's insight came from the deficiencies of Legal Realism, the persuasion to which he was converted at Yale, and which he then had the opportunity to test and refract in the powerfully formative experience serving in the government during the war.

One of Realism's patron saints, Holmes, had said that "the practice of law is nothing more pretentious that the prediction of what courts will in fact do." Legal Realists demonstrated that predictions about the future decisions of courts could never be made on the basis of text—black-letter law—alone and many of them scurried off in different directions in search of a silver bullet, a contextual factor that would provide the key to predicting the future. Returning to New Haven after the war, McDougal understood that the Realists were making six major mistakes.

First, in their search for predicting how decisions would be made, they were still locked in the essential passivity of Positivism. They were *predicting* what someone else would do. But McDougal understood that a critical part of jurisprudence's calling was to actively assist decision makers, by helping to clarify goals, provide information about means, the aggregate consequences of different options, and so on.

Second, in their focus on courts or the application of law, Realists were ignoring all the components of decision—pre-law making, law-making, law-terminating, law appraisal—that preceded and followed courts and other institutions of application. But McDougal understood from his governmental experience that these other functions are indispensable parts of understanding and practicing law.

Third, in their focus on law, Realists were overlooking what political and legal struggles were about: life opportunities or "values." They had no systematic way of designating and studying their production and distribution through time.

Fourth, in their focus on legal institutions, Realists were giving insufficient attention to the continuing impact of the rich dynamism of context and, in particular, to the role of power on decisions. As one of Harry Hopkins' hatchetmen in the Roosevelt Administration, McDougal came to understand that very well.

Fifth, in their focus on legal institutions, Realists did not grasp that the maintenance or adjustment of the institutions themselves was part of every decision and that the "institutions and structures," as political scientists called them, were products of an ongoing constitutive process.

Sixth, in their focus on the United States, Realists were ignoring the inevitable global dimension of influence and impact of apparently local decisions.

The Copernican Revolution in McDougal's jurisprudence was in unseating rules as the mechanism of decision and installing the human being—all human beings, to varying degrees—as deciders. But this was not a libertarian or *laisser faire* approach. Because McDougal committed himself to developing a theory about law that could establish and sustain a free society, he was not content with some so-called theory of rational choice by means of which individuals, deliriously libidinalized with greed, might pursue private interests on the happy assumption that, in the end, the great Invisible Hand would sort everything out for the best. The global depression and World War II had demonstrated that didn't work. McDougal's aspiration was always wider, enhanced and responsible participation in community decision in the common interest. As he wrote in May, 1997, in the last formal statement of his theory:

> the most useful conception of law is as a process of decision that is both authoritative and controlling. The function of the responsible jurist, advisor or decision-maker, who is a part of that process, is to develop an appropriate observational standpoint, clarify community goals, identify and then perform the intellectual tasks that will enable him or her to assist those who seek legal or policy advice in clarifying goals, and in implementing them in ways compatible with the common interests of the most inclusive community.[1]

You will note that, even in this final statement, McDougal focused on categories and conceptions. If law was not a body of rules, but a process of community decision and McDougal's goal was to enhance the operation of and participation in that process so that it contributed to the establishment of a public order of human dignity, the conceptual tools he could invent or adapt would be of critical importance. McDougal accepted Kant's notion of the centrality of categories of perception and he set about to consciously devise categories that were, in Morison's words, "deliberately and pragmatically chosen for the purposes in view."[2] Once McDougal had established his own categories, he devoted a great deal of time to understanding and critiquing the categories of contemporaries, precisely because he believed categories are central to the jurisprudential enterprise. Some of McDougal's students thought the explicit presentation and adaptation of the "scaffolding" was not necessary for every problem. He was convinced that it was.

Take observational standpoint. When a student in one of his classes made some judgmental or appraisal statement, McDougal was likely to ask: "who are you?" By that, he didn't mean 'what's your name' or 'who authorized you' and it was certainly not an invitation to a Cartesian exercise by means of which

---

[1] Preface to the Student Edition, Harold D. Lasswell & Myres S. McDougal, *Jurisprudence for a Free Society*, v (1997).

[2] William Morison, "Myres S. McDougal and Twentieth-Century Jurisprudence: A Comparative Essay," in Michael Reisman & Burns H. Weston, *Toward World Order and Human Dignity: Essays in Honor of Myres S. McDougal* 3 (1976).

the mere act of your cogitation is supposed to assuage your anxiety about your existence and hurry you past the relevant question of which one of the "yous" was momentarily engaged. Drawing on the philosophy of science, McDougal understood that the momentarily dominant self in your bundle of identities, at that moment in time, or 'history,' if you prefer, will perceive and appraise differently from other selves and that self-awareness and consistency in observation are critical preconditions to the success of every other intellectual task. For the foreign student and the minority student in classes at Yale listening to unself-conscious exponents of American viewpoints spout forth from lectern and floor, the "who-are-you" question made a lot of sense and it was a relief to hear a professor express and understand it. But establishing and then consistently maintaining an observational standpoint throughout an intellectual operation and, in particular, clarifying a standpoint that assists in discerning and realizing the common interest—the standpoint of "citizens of the larger community of mankind"—was no easy task.

As important as "who are you?" is how you look at things and what you decide to look at. The Realists and, even more, the sociological jurists had, of course, said that the social process is important and the jurist has to look at it. Max Weber and Roscoe Pound had devised ways of looking at more than economics. McDougal stood alone, however, in insisting on a systematic way of gathering and organizing information about the comprehensive social process and, even more important, on the clearest design of the lenses through which the jurist looked—lenses that could distinguish between perspectives and operations, authority and control, constitutive and public order decisions and so on. The division of things people want or "desired events" into eight, empirically-referential value categories proved to be an important tool in this regard. Once McDougal embarked on the task, his extraordinary demand for precision led him to identify within the social process, community process, power process, the constitutive process and the critical components that compose a decision, many of which jurisprudential analysis was ignoring.

Because McDougal had set the individual person at the center of law, how that person decided—or made choices—became a critical focus of his jurisprudence. Hence the identification and elaboration, in Aristotilean fashion, of the critical intellectual tasks of decision: goals, trends, conditions, projections, invention of alternatives. This is an aspect of McDougal's jurisprudence that is unique among his contemporaries, even those of the utilitarian persuasion, which is puzzling, because it is what law is all about.

It is surprising that the most controversial aspect of McDougal's jurisprudence was his insistence that the end of law and the criterion for appraisal of particular decisions was their degree of contribution to the achievement of a public order of human dignity. Curiously, the charge that these were "American" values almost always came from Americans and almost always angered McDougal's foreign students and collaborators. I recall Eisuke Suzuki from Japan, bounding out of his chair in fury. "How dare anyone suggest," he said, "that America invented the concept of human dignity." McDougal chuckled.

In May, 1997, at the ripe age of 91, McDougal wrote what proved to be the valedictory statement of his enterprise and its aspiration. He said:

> The highest calling of all is to enhance human dignity in appropriate systems of public order. For those in the next generation who share this goal, Lasswell and I hope that our work may prove useful in providing principles of content and procedure and the tools for implementing them.[3]

Did he succeed in this aspiration? Over the years, McDougal's image evolved in the collective mind of the academy and the profession from enfant terrible and destroyer of the law to elder statesman and prophet of human dignity. In international law, the field in which his theory was most often applied, his writings are now considered classic and are routinely cited, but they are often in those pretentious style citations, along with the *de rigeur* references to Grotius, Pufendorf or Vattel. In their study of how revolutionary political ideas diffuse, he and Lasswell called this "rejection by partial incorporation." But in looking for explicit references, I think McDougal, this once, may have used the wrong lens. His work has pervaded professional consciousness to the point where we may say, as Auden said in his eulogy of Freud, that "he is no more a person / Now but a whole climate of opinion / Under whom we conduct our differing lives."

---

[3] *Id.* at vi.

LUTHER L. McDOUGAL III
W. R. Irby Professor, Tulane University, School of Law

In his famous article with Harold Lasswell on legal education and public policy, Myres McDougal hinted that his first major book might be a property casebook. At one point the article states "[T]he organizing foci of the 'property' courses are such concepts as 'easement,' 'profit,' 'license,' 'covenant,' 'servitude,' or 'land contract,' 'deed,' 'delivery,' 'covenant of title,' or 'reversion,' 'possibility of reverter,' 'right of entry,' 'remainder,' and 'executory interest,' and not such goals as the provision of healthful housing, in well-planned communities, for all citizens at prices that they can afford to pay or the promotion of the cheap, secure, and speedy transfer of land, without adventitious restraints having no basis in policy, or the appraisal of doctrines and practices about the transmission of wealth from generation to generation in terms of their effects on a balanced distribution of claims in society." He expands on these ideas later in the article. I say he because Lasswell knew relatively little about property law. Five years later in 1948, he and David Haber published *Property, Wealth, Land: Allocation, Planning and Development*, which incorporates his thoughts in the article plus much more. This casebook represented a radical departure from the traditional mold both in terms of organization and content. It contained both original writings and excerpts from other works putting property law in its economic and social context. The casebook changed not only property law and the organization and content of future property casebooks but also the content of most future law school casebooks. Casebooks with social science materials are probably the norm today.

The law of property that the young Myres McDougal studied was still largely based on English common law and the focus, for the most part, was individualistic, the law being concerned with protecting the rights of property holders and, through the complexities of future interests, enhancing the individual's power to control his property from the grave. Considerations of public policy, to the limited extent they were considered, were largely concerned with protection of the individual's right to private property. This notion of relevant public policy probably resonated with the young Myres McDougal's own experience while growing up in rural Mississippi. His father, a doctor, acquired a good deal of land and, in general, land was viewed as the most important form of wealth and the basis for enhanced status in society. The casebooks that were used at Ole Miss, where Myres McDougal first studied property reflected these basic ideas. Although I don't know which casebook was used in his property course, a look at casebooks generally in use throughout the country at that time shows that they were primarily a collection of cases, many of them old English cases, with an occasional note that contained a list of supporting authority or a brief doctrinal statement expanding on what the court discussed in the principal case. Although Myres studied property again at Oxford, it is unlikely that any of the doctrines or the implicit policies were seriously challenged there because the study of law there was in the classical, historical and doctrinal mode.

At Yale, the young McDougal was forced to reassess many of his ideas. Wesley Newcomb Hohfeld had provided a powerfully destructive tool for the Legal Realists, and McDougal was particularly enchanted with the possibility of demonstrating that the law of future interests, in which he had excelled, was essentially a network of word games in which the words themselves were genetically imprecise. But if the Realist provided young McDougal with the tools for destroying the inherited doctrines, they did little to provide him with a means for building an alternative system. His meeting with Harold Lasswell and subsequent collaboration with him to develop an alternative system is well known. But another individual, Maurice Rotival, a French planner, also highly influenced McDougal in the property area. Rotival had worked in many places in the world, but settled in Connecticut and played a major role in regional planning in Connecticut. McDougal and Rotival became close friends and together published a book on regional planning in 1947. Lawyers and planners today could learn a lot about meaningful and effective regional planning from this relatively brief, but insightful book.

Insights he obtained from both Lasswell and Rotival provided McDougal, now a property law professor at Yale, a way of viewing the aggregate of a community's spatial resources through the prism of the law and to conceive of law's contribution as developing a rational method for utilizing those resources in ways that served common interests. The first edition of the casebook, which dramatically veered away from the traditional doctrinal organization of property casebooks, was organized in three major parts: Part I dealt with the basic notions of Property and Wealth, Part II covered Land (Resource) Allocation by Private Volition, and Part III explored Land Planning and Development. This organization alone permitted professors and students to gain new insights into what property law was really all about.

The introduction in Chapter 1 set the tone for the entire book. First, it defined property, wealth and land: "Property is commonly regarded as an institution (pattern of practices), wealth as a value (goods and services), and land as a resource (potential value)." These definitions are far different from those provided in most property books that are usually in terms of bundles of rights. Much of the rest of the introduction raised questions that the authors thought the materials in the book would help answer and which they hoped professors and students would explore when using the casebook. A few examples are: "By what specific practices and doctrines are resources allocated, planned, developed, and exploited in the United States today?" "Behind the formal façade of authority, what is the structure of real and effective control over important decisions about how resources are allocated, planned, developed and exploited?" "What values do the people of the United States demand today from their resources and institutions and by what procedures can these values be translated into concrete programs of action and specific objectives toward which property doctrines and practice may be directed?"

In addition to the Introduction to Chapter i, each chapter had an introduction that put the materials in the chapter in a policy perspective. My favorite is the introduction to Chapter III entitled "Dead Hand Volition: Trusts, Future Interests, Possessory Estates." Selected quotes reveal the general flavor of this introduction. " [The] projection of dead hand control over resources and wealth is a part, though not an invariable or indispensable part, of that continuing process, or flow of events, by which in our society wealth is transmitted from generation to generation, and it cannot be understood or appraised, for policy purposes, except as a part of that process or flow of events." Then later in the introduction they state: "The traditional categorization of possessory estates and future interests—that great structure of doctrinal nebulae: reversions, rights of entry, possibilities of reverter, vested remainders, contingent remainders, and executory interests—developed in an England of aristocratic family dynasties and primogeniture, when the maintenance of feudal dues and seisin were still important, when competition between the courts of Chancery and of Common Law was most severe, when modes of conveyancing were still primitive and formal, and before the community had developed generalized notions of freedom of contract and private volition. It needs no emphasis that the conditions, which may have at one time made these distinctions rational efforts to implement community policies, have long since disappeared. It will bear emphasis, however, that these distinctions linger on as irrational verbalisms, making shifting and ambiguous references to the whole range of very different contemporary problems."

As one might imagine the casebook received mixed reviews. Some professors considered it a major break through in the way property should be taught. Others were far less enthusiastic. Professor W. Barton Leach, a well-known property professor from an institution north of here, had the following to say, after observing that all property professors who examine the book would be enriched by the "originality and vitality of the book": "The use of this book in a *first-year* law course strikes me as impossible unless one is prepared to forfeit those things which I think of as professional standards of treatment. The emphasis of the book is upon evaluation of our system of property on the basis of its attainment of sociological and political values. It is clear to me that this cannot be engaged in at a professional level unless the student has a deep knowledge of the system he is criticizing, of the interrelation of its principles, of the courses of self-correction within itself, and of how the thing actually works and is used.... It may also be that it is not the best way to lead a young man into thorough understanding of a system to keep saying to him, 'This is silly. There is no vision. People do not know what they are doing. The whole thing is wrong, wrong, WRONG!!!' I am well aware of how often impossibilities prove to be chimeras, particularly in the field of education; but experiments should not be tried by those who think them improbable of success. McDougal has got to try this one, not I."

Adverse reaction to the casebook was not limited to academia. The legislatures of three states passed statutes or resolutions that prohibited the use of the casebook in law schools in the state. They did so on the basis that the casebook was espousing communism. This, of course, showed a complete misunderstanding of the book and what Myres McDougal was all about. From the earliest day as an educator he was an advocate of a free democratic society, and the thought of government owning all land and the means of production was the furthest thing from his mind. Although the casebook explored increased governmental intervention into the various patterns of practices constituting the notion of property, the end it sought to achieve was the removal of ancient concepts that prevented the legal process from serving the needs of the social process. Many of the controls he discussed, particularly those relating to land-use planning unheard of in 1948, have now become common place and have made the communities in which they have been implemented better places to live.

With these negative reactions aside, the reception of McDougal's book in the United States was astonishing. It is clear that the book marked a fundamental change in the way that American lawyers and law teachers would henceforth look at the area of property. A look at the property books available today reveals that most of them contain some, if not many, themes that are found in his casebook. The book can plainly be considered, not simply the initiator of new ways of studying property, but also the foundation for new courses in land-use planning and environmental law as well. No question exists in my mind, that McDougal's work on property provided him with the kernel that became his law of the oceans and subsequently his law of outer space. The latter was written at a time when the possibilities of using space still seemed fantastic, more a subject for movies and television than for a law book. This book caused many of McDougal's friends and students to loom that this time the poor man has gone too far! They simply miscalculated how great Myres McDougal's vision was.

I first used *Property, Wealth and Land* the first year I taught property at Ole Miss in 1967. It was the perfect extension of what I consider the best intellectual experience I ever had in school, my year at Yale working on my LL.M. I had taken almost all of the courses Myres taught and had become an advocate of policy-oriented jurisprudence. Unlike Professor Leach's fears of what would happen to students exposed to the casebook, I found that students gained a better understanding of the traditional doctrines once they learned their limitations and considered relevant contemporary community policies. I continued using the book when I started teaching at the University of Arizona, but I had to stop using it because the publisher ran out of printed copies. I was forced to use other property casebooks for a while. I tried several and found them all lacking in organization and policy analysis. I mentioned the problem to Myres, and he suggested the possibility of a second edition of *Property, Wealth and Land*. After some discussions with the publisher and a determination that David Haber was not interested in participating in a new edition, we decided to begin working on the new edition.

After several months, I finally had a draft of the second edition completed. I sent it to Myres, and he then suggested that I come to New Haven for about a week so we could go over the book. This I did, and we worked on the book morning, noon and night. This was the most invigorating intellectual experience I have ever had. He raised question after question, he posed policy issue after policy issue, he constantly questioned whether what we were saying conveyed the exact thoughts we wanted to convey, and, perhaps most surprising to me, was his frequent questioning of some doctrinal statements. I say it was surprising to me because it had been many years since he had taught property, yet he remember doctrinal details that most people would have long ago forgotten. Because I had been a student of his and had read most of his writings, I already knew that he was a great mind and scholar, but until I spent a week working with him I did not fully appreciate how great he really was.

FLORENTINO P. FELICIANO
Member, Appellate Body, World Trade Organization, Geneva, Switzerland

MAINTENANCE OF MINIMUM WORLD PUBLIC ORDER

It was an act of courage on the part of Myres S. McDougal to undertake, in the 1950's, a book about the law of war. It was the height of the Cold War. Large numbers of nuclear weapons were poised to destroy the United States and the Soviet Union, and much of the rest of humanity. The clock of the Bulletin of Atomic Scientists read two minutes to midnight. Public perception of the danger was acute. School children in the United States were undergoing, not the ordinary fire drills, but nuclear attack drills. People were building bomb shelters in their backyards, underneath the barbecue grills.

When we began our study, scholarship on the law of war was almost evenly divided between two camps. One camp, the Realists, assumed that a law of war had become impossible. A very distinguished Belgian jurist, Charles de Visscher, in his influential "Theory and Reality in Public International Law," counseled his academic colleagues:

> The new weapons of mass destruction have revolutionized all data of war, and it is above all for this reason that the jurists will be well advised to waste no further time in what some of them still persist in calling the "Restatement" of the Laws of War. To try to adapt these laws to the new conditions is not only labor absolutely lost; it is an enterprise that in certain of its aspects may be dangerous.
>
> ...There is better work to be done today than picking up the fragments of an obsolete body of rules.[1]

The other camp was composed of equally distinguished and deeply committed, but perhaps somewhat romantic, scholars. These scholars assembled formulations of rules enumerated over the last one and a half centuries and attempted to weave them into a coherent set of propositions that somehow, they hoped, would restrain top political and military leaders and battlefield commanders. Precisely because the issues involved were so important to the future of mankind, Myres McDougal identified this subject for the first of a series of treatises on international law that he was projecting. I had the honor, which I have treasured throughout my life, of being invited to collaborate with

---

[1] Charles de Visscher, "Theory and Reality in Public International Law," 293 *quoted in* Myres S. McDougal & Florentino P. Feliciano, *Law and Minimum Public Order: The Legal Regulation of International Coercion* 3 (1961).

him on the project. My preparation was limited. I had read the Hague Conventions of 1899 and 1907 and the Geneva 1929 Prisoners of War Convention during my undergraduate days in the law school of the University of the Philippines. However, my experience during the belligerent occupation of the Philippines by Japan during the Second World War had not inspired a deep faith in the efficacy of this law.

We started our work with no illusion. We assumed nothing—certainly not the basic premise of other scholars that war and peace had to be distinguished sharply since each state or condition of things had attached to it a separate corpus of rules—the law of peace and the law of war—that operated successively, at different times, one to the exclusion of the other. We understood that whether the terms "war" and "peace"; "low intensity conflict" and "peace"; or "no war, no peace," were used or not by legislators, administrators, or judges, nation-states exercised against each other a continuously varying degree of coercion—that coercion may range from a very low, perhaps negligible level, in which case we spoke of influence in basically consensual types of political and economic situations, all the way to the opposite pole of very intense applications of military violence resulting in more or less widespread destruction of human life and property and environment. A treatise that sought to grapple with these factual processes across state boundaries, would have to be organized quite differently from the standard texts.

At the outset, therefore, we described in comprehensive terms those phases of interaction across state boundaries which are marked by a relatively high degree of coercion exercised with a relatively extensive destruction of human life and other human values. We also described the processes of decision-making in which authoritative or legal norms were thought to play some role, by which processes the international community sought to control, regulate, or mitigate the processes of force and violence. We identified the major types of controversies which posed common or related issues of policy and which are addressed by various officials—executive, military, or judicial—located in various levels and phases of the continuous processes by which authoritative decisions are made and implemented. The central aspect of our enterprise was the effort to articulate and clarify the essential principles of minimum or basic order—that is to say, the principles indispensable for achieving that minimum of public order without which the bonds of society break apart and there is only the darkness of chaos and the war of each against all others.

When recourse to force does occur, the community policies needed to reduce to a minimum the destruction of life and other human values, also need to be clarified and examined in detail. We reviewed the scholarly literature in detail and discovered that much of the learning and rhetoric in use did not contribute significantly to intellectual clarification or to identification of the necessary policies.

We appreciated that one of the most difficult problems in the field was that of distinguishing between lawful and unlawful resort to intense coercion, *i.e.,* military force or violence. This had been a recurring problem in the application of the law of war for centuries, and had become a frontline problem when the United Nations Charter was promulgated at the end of the Second World War. We rejected "brightline" formulations or catchy phrases that seemed to permit a decision-maker, with apparent ease, to decide quickly whether particular exercises of coercion, especially intense coercion, were lawful or unlawful. Instead, considering the complexities in the trans-border applications of coercion, and especially the difficulties of objective fact-finding in international relations, we suggested a framework and modes of explicit, systematic, and contextual examination of applications of force and violence, and appraised those in terms of goals of the community of nations, short-term and long-term goals, before concluding that particular uses of coercion were lawful or not.

One of the most important functions of an organized community is the initiation and management of sanctions in order to secure the implementation of law in respect of resort to force, as well as law about particular exercises of force. We examined the arsenal of instruments available to the international community and, more important in my view, we analyzed the various strategic objectives of sanctions operations.

We examined as well the issues of neutrality in the world where the United Nations Charter had been promulgated, but whose levels of commitment had already begun to be eroded.

We also explored the law of war in actual combat situations. Here we sought to develop sets of criteria that could assist a decision-maker (whether a battlefield commander or a judge of a court-martial or of a war crimes tribunal) in addressing such questions as who are permissible combatants; which weapons were permissible in what types of situations to achieve what levels of destruction. I believe we were among the earliest to observe that the law of war in combat situations is in fact the law of human rights in armed conflict situations.

Finally, we explored in detail the complex subject of belligerent occupation, a subject whose recurrent importance we had not contemplated at that time, though in recent times, it is as contemporary as the wars in the Persian Gulf, Bosnia-Herzegovina, Kosovo, and the Congo.

The reception of *Law and Minimum World Public Order: The Legal Regulation of International Coercion* was itself an interesting story. The book promptly became a *vade mecum* in ministries of defense in many countries. Its utility for national war colleges and legal advisers to defense and foreign affairs ministries derived as much from the comprehensiveness and thoroughness of the detailed examination of the legal instruments and doctrinal literature as well as case law on the subject, as from the method of thinking about problems that it offered. In the Department of Defense at the United States, I have it on good authority that Mac became something of a hero. Mac himself, however, admitted only that after our book came out, he became a private consultant to the Joint Chiefs of Staff and served as such for a substantial period of time. In the then Soviet bloc countries, the book was analyzed in detail and frequently criticized but I was told that certain approaches taken in subsequent Soviet bloc literature indicated that that literature was not completely immune from our book's influence. I leave it to you to decide whether that was a commendable thing or not. What I can testify from personal experience was that some of our basic concepts—those relating to management of combat operations and to belligerent occupation—find reflection in the Two Additional Protocols of 1977 to the Geneva Conventions of 1949. Indeed some of the language of Protocol One sounds remarkably similar to language found in certain chapters of our book. After the 1977 Protocols were adopted by the intergovernmental conference, I suggested to Mac that at long last, the book and we had become respectable.

Looking back over almost forty years since the book has been published, I think it is clear that the approach that we developed with respect to determining the lawfulness of weapon selection and application in combat situations has become the standard mode of analysis. Our theory of sanctions, which I believe is a distinctive contribution to the jurisprudential literature, is now reflected in the many appraisals of war crimes tribunals, truth and reconciliation commissions, compensation commissions and other institutional means for dealing with grave violations of the law of war for and stitching together the social fabric that armed conflict tears asunder. Our analysis of aggression and neutrality, however, seems to have been largely overtaken by time and global political developments. Despite the general language of the collective security system in the United Nations Charter and its virtual universality, states seem unwilling to accept the obligations that it necessarily entails. Professor McDougal would very probably have thought that there will yet be a sad price to pay for this backing away from law and I fear that he would be correct.

This brief account of the impact that Myres McDougal had on the law of war would be incomplete if I did not mention the impact he had on a young student from the Philippines who had come to Yale for graduate education. That young student could hardly have anticipated that he would be befriended by this towering figure in international law, made into a collaborator and that the Professor would stand by as a warm and committed personal friend and father-figure, and a caring friend of my own children, for a lifetime. Most if not all of the important things which have happened to me in the course of my own career in the law have been in some way or another, connected to collaboration with, and the teaching and friendship of Myres McDougal.

LUNG-CHU CHEN

Professor, New York Law School; Research Affiliate in Law, Yale Law School
President, New Century Foundation, Taipei, Taiwan

CHAMPION FOR AN INTERNATIONAL LAW OF HUMAN DIGNITY

"Lung-chu, we have come a long way together." Those are the last words Mac said to me when I returned from Taiwan and visited with him last March, holding his hand at his bed side. Yes, Mac, we have come a long way together since 1960 when I first met you in Taiwan as a young law school graduate. For the past thirty-eight years, from Taiwan to the United States, to Yale, to New York Law School, and to all points in between, Professor Myres McDougal has been a great mentor, teacher, and counselor.

First and foremost, Mac has been a wonderful personal and family friend. When my wife Judy and I were married in 1967, Mac, together with Harold Lasswell, gave us a wedding reception at the New Haven Lawn Club, and wished us, in his words, "an optimum shaping and sharing of affection and all other values in pursuit of both public and civic order." I am also proud to say that there is a McDougal in my family, Eleanor McDougal Chen, Mac's god daughter, who takes pride in her middle name. In the good old days, it was customary for the Chens to pay the McDougals an annual visit during the Christmas holiday season, and those visits were among my family's happiest moments. Mac, Mrs. McDougal, and John were the most gracious of hosts. My family and I will miss Mac dearly.

I had the distinct privilege to be invited by Mac and Harold Lasswell to co-author the treatise on *Human Rights and World Public Order*. As I had been their student and co-author with Harold of a previous book, *Formosa, China, and the United Nations,* I was conversant with their policy science approach, otherwise known as the Yale School or New Haven School of International Law. Writing the human rights book with them has been a central part of my professional life. It was an experience that transformed me.

I would like to describe briefly the state of art at the time we began the human rights project nearly three decades ago: how Myres McDougal conceived the project, his goals, the method he employed, and the impact it has had on subsequent scholarship and on international protection of human rights.

When we began to survey the field at that time, we were struck by the inadequacies that were plainly apparent in the existing human rights literature. Mac characterized it as "simple intellectual confusion." The concept of human rights was often left obscure, or simply taken for granted without any discussion at all. Little effort had been made to create a comprehensive map of the totality of human rights, and there had been little discussion of the detailed content of particular rights. Some of the writings were highly anecdotal and emotive. The principal focus of this vast and confused literature had been what was called the problem of implementation. Even with this problem, however, the range of alternatives considered had been highly partial and fragmented. Most recommendations for improvement in implementation had been upon isolated features of rule and procedure. They ignored the processes of author-itative decision and effective power which impacted all changes in rules and procedures. In addition, there was a conspicuous lack of a systematic problem-solving approach that would employ all relevant intellectual skills. And finally, the subject of human rights was particularly challenging because of multi-cul-turalism and profound philosophical, religious, and political cleavages in the world community.

To confront this challenge, McDougal wanted to provide a comprehensive intellectual framework of inquiry that simply could not be achieved by the arbitrary groupings of subject topics in the traditional fashion, or by anecdotal, emotive approaches. He wanted to undertake a systematic, philosophical reconsideration of the goals of human dignity. He wanted to specify human rights by identifying empirically referential claims for protection and fulfillment of values. Values are preferred events—what people cherish. The content of human rights is, in essence, the shaping and sharing of all values—respect, power, enlightenment, well-being, wealth, skill, affection, and rectitude.

For each claim, in his customary fashion, Mac wanted to clarify community goals, to survey trends of past decision and practice, to analyze conditioning factors, to project likely patterns of future development, and to invent and rec-ommend alternatives for improvement. Mac conceived the concept of human rights broadly; he underscored the interdependence of all human rights; he systematically spelled out the preferred community policy for each claim; he devised the principles of content and procedure as guides for resolving conflicting claims for protection and fulfillment of values; he related the mea-sures of implementation to the world constitutive process of authoritative decision and to effective global power process; and he emphasized the dynamic interplay of international law and politics.

The volume that I had the privilege of working on, and which Mac has bequeathed to us, stands as the most systematic and intellectually rigorous treatment of international human rights law. The first half of the volume, as described above, sets forth a general framework for dealing systematically with all human rights, and the second half is concerned with the *respect* value.

Mac believed *respect* was the core value of human rights. This core value concerns the honoring of "each other's freedom of choice about participation in other value processes." Thus respect entails the freedom of choice that is inherent in the dignity and worth of every human being, equality in both the positive and negative sense, and recognition for contributing to the common interest. Claims about participation in different value processes, asserted with varying degrees of intensity, occupy a central place in the defense and fulfillment of human rights.

In keeping with his grand vision and design, Mac had hoped to do eight volumes on human rights, elaborating in detail each of the eight values: respect, power, enlightenment, well-being, wealth, skill, affection, and rectitude. I only wish I had eight lives!

Mac practiced what he preached. The human rights book meant so much to him because it afforded him the opportunity to develop the overriding concept of human dignity which was central to his commitment and jurisprudence for a free society. He worked on the treatise day and night: we met at his office almost daily—weekends included. There was a time he and I called each other "the slave driver." We discontinued that affectionate indulgence after completing the section on the eradication of slavery and its equivalent practices. Mac always worked with passion, especially in connection with the topic of age-based discrimination. He was emphatic in his conviction that mandatory retirement based on the calendar year was simply barbaric. The chapter on "The Protection of the Aged from Discrimination" is the eloquent testimony to this conviction.

This year humankind is commemorating the 50th Anniversary of the Universal Declaration of Human Rights. Fifty years ago, the adoption of the Universal Declaration by United Nations General Assembly set off within the United States a violent reaction led by the then President of the American Bar Association. Myres McDougal, as an early human rights activist, rose to the occasion and defended the Universal Declaration by publishing a powerful monograph in the Yale Law Journal. And long before Jimmy Carter's human rights diplomacy, Mac had introduced the subject of international protection of human rights to law school curricula and helped to place it on the intellectual landscape through his writings and speeches.

Today, human rights have emerged as the spinal column of the United Nations era: we judge the legitimacy of a government by whether it lives up to the international standards of human rights. In the meantime, the human rights industry—academic, activist, or otherwise—has flourished. Nation-states, international governmental organizations, non-governmental organizations and private associations, and individual persons all have important roles to play in the defense and fulfillment of human rights.

Professor Frank Turner, a former provost of Yale, once asked me: "Is it true that Myres McDougal is the greatest international lawyer since Hugo Grotius, the founding father of international law?" Of course, he was. It was a rare honor and privilege and a constant source of inspiration to work with the greatest international lawyer of all time. Mac, you are and will be dearly missed.

DAME ROSALYN HIGGINS

Judge, International Court of Justice, The Hague, The Netherlands

McDOUGAL AS TEACHER, MENTOR, AND FRIEND

Myres McDougal was an inspired teacher whose deeply original ideas have irrevocably altered the way we think about international law. No international lawyer of the last fifty years has been so much written about by others. His pugnacious style on matters legal was matched by Southern courtesy on matters personal. He was adored by his students and liked and respected even by those who profoundly disagreed with him.

Beyond any question at all, Myres McDougal has been the greatest teacher of international law in the post-war world. This is not to denigrate other fine teachers, of whom, happily, there are many. I, like most of us, developed under and benefited from several exceptional teachers, each with their particular skills.

But there is no denying that Mac was in a class of his own when it came to teaching. The revolutionary ideas, combined with the power of his oversize personality, left none of his students untouched. Today we speak of the "charisma" of certain leaders. But it is the wrong word to describe Mac, because the image is of someone whose deeply attractive personality moves an audience to follow where he leads. That was not at all the process with Mac. What we felt, rather, was that upon arrival at Yale we were simply blown down by a hurricane whose nature we did not yet comprehend, left for a period to dust ourselves down, and then invited to continue a journey together.

I came to Yale in 1959, after taking two degrees in law at Cambridge. For the first few weeks I was, quite simply, shell shocked. I thought I knew a lot of international law and probably, for a student, I did. But I had no idea whatever about what it was all *for,* nor that legal judgments were not necessarily "givens," but could be intellectually challenged by scholars—and indeed even by students. The language of the McDougal-Lasswell policy science approach was, quite simply, incomprehensible. Sir Robert Jennings, my Cambridge teacher and later British Judge at the International Court, has reminded me on more than one occasion that I wrote to him asking how he could have let me choose Yale over Harvard as the place to pursue my studies. I had totally lost my bearings, because the inadequacy of what I came equipped with was being demonstrated to me in ruthless fashion, before I really understood what the proffered alternative was.

Mac's pedalogical technique, then, was to throw you in the deep end and, if you survived at all, to show you how to make waves. The Socratic teaching method (which also was quite unfamiliar to me, as I had been taught by lectures coupled with gentle, private, tutorial discussion) ensured that you made the journey yourself. That journey was to an international law that was not rules but process, and was not neutral but dedicated to the achievement of specified social ends. The journey was tumultuous, but for those of us who made it with Mac, the inner and intellectual rewards have been great. Those two great themes—process and social purpose—remain my lodestars today. And this is true of countless others around the world.

He was also a role model to generations of students. Today that phrase, "role model," has come to be associated with persons whose gender, race or religion is not that of the power structures in the society in question. Their achievements, often in the face of seemingly insurmountable obstacles, is thus the more impressive and inspirational for young people of the same sexual, religious or racial identity. They see from the role model what they, too, can do.

Myres McDougal was white, male and from a southern Methodist background—hardly a minority icon and certainly not an endangered species. But he was undeniably a role model. He was a role model in the sense that the way he did things was imprinted on the students at Yale who were to be the next generation of teachers. A role model shows by example. Mac showed that you don't have to choose between being an outstanding scholar and a caring teacher. All too often great scholars treat teaching as a chore to be endured, as an intrusion on what they really want to do. But those of us who were at Yale during the era of Myres McDougal learned by osmosis the deep truth that absorption of knowledge, the creation of ideas and their imparting to the next generation are a seamless unity. These are not alternatives to be selected among at will. There is a duty—a pleasing, fulfilling duty—to wear the mantles of scholar and teacher simultaneously.

And so it was that, during those very decades when Mac was at his most productive, writing path-breaking volumes of great importance, he was nonetheless always available to his students. Knocking on the door of his office at Yale Law School one would hear the shouted command "Come!" (*never* "Come in"). When one had entered the room, an imposing figure wearing a green eye visor could eventually be discerned among the thousands of books which filled all available space. No student ever felt rushed. Indeed, the lucky ones might be invited to the Graduate Club to continue the discussion over dinner.

Our theses were properly supervised—every word had been read, our teacher expected detailed discussion, and apparently relished it. He gave of his time willingly, with an 'open door' policy even at the height of his scholarly activity and legal consulting.

Mac's significance as a role model in international law has thus had its significance not just in his intellectual ideas but in the realm of teaching. The fact that today, all over the world, there are former students of Mac's, now caring for *their* students, listening to their concerns, encouraging their endeavours, is part of his inheritance to the international community.

Myres McDougal was our mentor, as well as our teacher. What is meant by this well-tried phrase? It means that the teacher not only imparts his knowledge and ideas, but tries to assist his students in their careers, to take an interest in their development. In this sense, most good teachers are also mentors to their students. But—as with so much of his life—this element too was writ large so far as McDougal was concerned. By some magical process, you could over twelve or more months have metamorphosized from baffled newcomer to someone thought by McDougal to have promise. And then his support as mentor knew no bounds. It mattered not—as I have good reason to know— that you might by now be three thousand, or six thousand miles away. You had become part of the invisible reality of the Yale policy science school, which school did not depend upon physical geography. Mac would write references more generous than one could hope for, pen supportive letters on one's behalf, go to extraordinary trouble to advance one's cause. All of this often went on unseen and unsolicited. We had moved, without fanfare, from student to friend, and now benefited from a friendship of the most intense warmth and generosity and loyalty.

There was another element that so many of us here today can attest to. Mac was zealous and active in supporting his students from this job or that honour. All of his formidable energies went into this. The addressee of his proposals was metaphorically backed against the wall and seized by the lapels. Mac did not hesitate to play the southern power-politician in support of his young colleagues, his former students.

His "former students" is, of course, an inept phrase altogether. He remained our teacher all of his life, even though we might have become professors, attorneys, government lawyers, judges. Of course, in the later years he inevitably became less familiar with the substance of the contemporary legal issues with which we might be exercised. He no longer followed, blow by blow, the ratification process of this or that treaty, the separate opinion of this or that judge, the text of this or that UN resolution. But his clarity of vision about what I will term "the McDougal-Lasswell" system remained undimmed, as did his ability to explain and expound and to relate it to legal problems that one might share with him. Above all, he never lost sight of the underlying value system. Notwithstanding age and increasing infirmity, he remained the very best person—as teacher, mentor and friend—to whom to turn in the face of any deep problem of principle or ethics.

We shall miss him dreadfully. Myres McDougal has left us with his ideas, our personal memories and the strong bonds of mutual support felt by all those who think of themselves as belonging to the Yale policy science school. This is indeed a legacy to celebrate.

PHOTOGRAPHS

Mr. Myres McDougal.

A CHARMED LIFE

Excerpts from a recorded conversation
with Judge Ronald St. J. Macdonald,
European Court of Human Rights,
August 7, 1995,
North Branford, Connecticut

I had not seen Myres McDougal for several years. I knew he was ill and I was determined not to let another summer go by without making an effort to visit him.

So on a torrid day in early August 1995 I took a plane from Halifax, Nova Scotia, to Boston, a train from Boston to New Haven, and the following morning, kindness of Professor Michael Reisman, a car to the Health Center at Evergreen Woods, the spacious and comfortable retirement community located in North Branford, Connecticut, about ten miles from New Haven, where Myres McDougal had been living since October, 1991.

Professor McDougal received me with the warmth and cordiality for which he is renowned. After a light lunch in the main dining area we adjourned to his private room where he stretched out on his bed, fully dressed, arms folded, legs crossed, eyes closed. He adjusted the Yale cap he wore throughout the time I was there and invited me to "ask anything you like."

Knowing that scholars would soon be writing in detail about his professional work—indeed they are well into it—I sought to keep the conversation personal.

Here then is an informal perspective of our good friend and inspiring colleague Myres McDougal...of the charmed life.

————

MACDONALD: What was it like growing up in rural Mississippi in the early years of the 20th century?

McDOUGAL: Well it was very exciting. I was born in a little town called Burton, in the northeast part of the state, on the Mobile and Ohio Railway. My father was a country doctor but he changed homes often. He would buy one house and then when he made a little money he would buy another house and this was in the town of Booneville about fifteen miles east of Burton. Booneville was really my home. My father practiced there for forty years. I grew up in Booneville and went to kindergarten and high school there. We had good schools and I had good teachers. I had one sweetheart the whole time and unhappily in my senior year she ran off with the son of the new Methodist minister but they never got married. I saw her in Memphis just a couple of years ago before she died and I told her she had made a great mistake and she said she understood it.

I drove the car for my father. I didn't even have to have a license to drive the car. People were very friendly. Race relations were much better than many people would assume. Our home was on the street that ended where the black community began and some of my earliest playmates were black playmates and we got along fine together; we didn't have any problems. Mississippi was a fine place to grow up in; the hunting was good, the fishing was good, and life in general was good, and I think it was good for the blacks too. Nobody ever went hungry or anything of that kind at least that I knew anything about and I think that I did know.

MACDONALD: What about life at Ole Miss? You said you taught Latin and Greek there.

McDOUGAL: My ability in Latin and Greek is due to a high school teacher, the wife of the superintendent of schools in Booneville, a lady a little out of her mind but a very good Latin scholar. I took everything she taught and she taught Latin. She took to me and said I could be very good, especially in Latin. So when I went to the University of Mississippi I was well prepared in Latin. The Latin teacher at the University of Mississippi was chairman of the Rhodes Scholarship Selection Committee and my father made certain that I took Latin. The professor of Greek was the dean of liberal arts at Ole Miss. At that time there were only four hundred students in the University of Mississippi as a whole. That number included the professional schools, the law school and the medical school. Four hundred students in the university as a whole. So we got almost tutorial instruction in subjects like Latin and Greek.

The professor of Greek was the dean and I had signed up for chemistry but the card kept coming back with chemistry marked out and Greek substituted. When this happened two or three times I finally acquiesced and took Greek and within two years I was teaching Greek. I held the rank of Instructor in the University. I was listed in the Faculty Bulletin. I taught both Latin and Greek to university students. So when I got to England I knew more Latin and Greek than most of the English boys knew.

MACDONALD: Were there any female students or mature students at Ole Miss in your time?

McDOUGAL: Young ladies were about a third of the student body and they were much sought after of course and I had good luck again. My mother's youngest brother lived in Oxford and one of the things he owned was a flower shop. So I always had plenty of flowers. I had free flowers for all my girlfriends, which made it very nice.

We had a great life at Ole Miss. There were many events on almost every weekend. We didn't have fraternities, we weren't supposed to have them, but we had them *sub rosa*. Ole Miss was a wonderful place to be. I discovered there that I could be pretty good.

Baseball was the big sport in those days and everybody played baseball or watched baseball. We also had football and basketball. I was much better in football and basketball than I was in baseball. We had the same amusements that I suppose people had in most of the country. There was a lot of hunting and fishing.

MACDONALD: So you enjoyed Ole Miss.

McDOUGAL: I did. Ole Miss was a wonderful place. It was close to Memphis. It was a very social place. We did not have fraternities but we had secret groups that became fraternities and we had dances almost every week. It was a lively place but the people also worked hard; they were good students and they had their rivalries. One of my classmates was later president of the American Bar Association, a man named John Satterfield, whom I beat for the Rhodes scholarship. That is an amusing story.

Satterfield and I lived in the same building and when they held the meeting of the Rhodes Scholarship Committee there were two Rhodes Scholars from Millsaps College in Jackson on the Committee and there were two from Southwestern University in Memphis. The chancellor of the University of Mississippi, Dr. Alfred P. Hume, was chairman of the Committee. I learned later that the two people from Millsaps voted for John Satterfield, the two people from Southwestern in Memphis voted for me, and Hume, the chancellor of the University of Mississippi, broke the tie in my favor.

Later I went to see him and I said, "Doctor, I greatly appreciate your not abstaining but breaking the tie in my favor." He said, "Mr. McDougal, when I needed a friend, you were my friend; I figured you needed a friend." What happened was that they had put one of those monkey bills through the state legislature and were trying to fire the Chancellor. I was editor-in-chief of the weekly paper *The Mississippian;* I published a special edition of the paper, took it down to Jackson, the state capital, and threatened to publicly defend the chancellor against the state legislature. That scared them off and for reasons I never understood they let him alone. He stayed on as chancellor. I thought the incident was sort of funny. He did not hesitate a moment; he said, "I figured you needed a friend."

Myres Smith McDougal

MACDONALD: How did you become interested in public international law?

McDOUGAL: In 1923 at the University of Mississippi the football coach, whom I greatly admired, wanted to be a scholar. The only subject the university would let him have was international law So in the fall of 1923 I studied international law under the direction of the football coach. This man, Kenneth P. Vinsel, was a much better teacher than he was a coach. He ended up as a professor of political science at the University of Louisville, where my father had been a medical student. Vinsel made me go back and read the works of the great founders of international law in their original words, often in Latin. He was an inspiring teacher. I really began with him.

When I went to England in 1927, international law was a required subject in the examinations and by great good luck I became a student of James L. Brierly who had just been made professor of international law, the Chichele Professor of International Law at Oxford. He had about one hundred students who would sit in a classroom and in the English style take down his lecture verbatim. Early in the fall of 1927 I was sitting at one of the desks on the aisle, putting my notes together, preparing to escape on my bicycle, when Brierly came striding down the alleyway, stopped beside my desk, and said, "You are an American, aren't you?" and I replied, "Yes sir, I am an American." He said, "Would you like to have lunch?" I said that I would be delighted to have lunch. So we had lunch together and from that day on we became close personal friends. He would have me out to his house on weekends to meet people and he even asked me to write special tutorials for him.

My tutor at Oxford was Sir William Holdsworth. He made me and Edmund Belsheim, the boy from North Dakota, with whom I shared rooms, write papers for him. When we finished he said, "I see you boys can write; from now on you will just come here and ask me questions." So while our fellow classmates were slaving over their tutorials we prepared questions and went and asked Holdsworth for the answers. Holdsworth had a good deal of respect for international law and he had no objection when Brierly wanted to give me tutorials. So I did go to Brierly for tutorials and Brierly was very rough with me. He did not like my language. I had taught Latin and Greek at Mississippi before going to Oxford and he would go through and cross out all my big words and cast them into short English words.

Brierly was a wonderful friend and I came to know him and his family and we remained friends as long as he lived. I do not think he ever got his due from the British government; he should have been given more senior employments than he got, and he felt that way. I visited him in 1950. We sat out in his garden under a tree and I asked him what he was doing and he looked at me and said, "Nothing." I had a sense then that he was dying and he was dead within a few months. He was a very great man and a very great inspiration; he meant as much to me as almost anybody I knew.

MACDONALD: Have I got it right then, the interest in international law was sparked by the football coach at Ole Miss and the Chichele Professor of International Law at Oxford? Not your usual combination.

McDOUGAL: Yes, that is correct; the two of them together. The football coach at Ole Miss turned out to be a very fine scholar. Of course Brierly never got his just desserts. He was a better scholar than Lauterpacht but he never got the recognition that Lauterpacht got. He was really a very great man, a great human being, and for an Englishman just beginning a new career to stop and ask an American student to have lunch was an extraordinary courtesy.

MACDONALD: Why did you decide to become an academic lawyer rather than, say, going into government service or the practice of law or seeking to enter public life perhaps as an elected representative from down south?

McDOUGAL: Sir William Holdsworth was the real cause of that. My Oxford room-mate, Edmund Belsheim, and I both took a first in the B.A. degree. Hugh Cox from Nebraska and I were the only two firsts in the B.C.L. Belsheim did not get a first in the B.C.L. but Holdsworth thought both of us should teach. He told me that I was better fitted for teaching than for Wall Street. Holdsworth had friends at Yale. He knew Charles Clark, dean of the Yale Law School and later a federal circuit judge, and he said, "I will send you to Yale and I will send Belsheim to Chicago," which he did. Belsheim later taught at Nebraska, became dean at Nebraska.

Holdsworth told me he wrote only one line to Clark at Yale and I said, "one line won't get me a fellowship there." Holdsworth, whom I had come to know very well—he had tea parties every Sunday—said, "the one line I wrote will get you there." I learned later that what he wrote was, "McDougal is the best student I have ever had," which I thought was a pretty high compliment.

Holdsworth had a great many American students over the years. He had a house on Grand Pothouse. Do you know where Grand Pot is at Oxford? There is a house on a little island just below the bridge and Holdsworth owned that house and had open house every Sunday with members of the Bar in attendance. He became very much like a father to me. Incidentally, his son was shot down during the war and Holdsworth became a very unhappy man; his wife was not a pleasant woman and she gave him a hard time after the boy was gone.

MACDONALD: Sir William Holdsworth was an eminent legal historian. Did he have an influence on you?

McDOUGAL: He had a tremendous influence on me not simply as an historian but because he knew almost everything. He could discuss any kind of a topic; he would raise all kinds of questions and discuss them. He had a fabulous memory, a photographic memory, and he knew where everything was. He just could reach up and pull down a book on anything he wanted to look up. He was a very cultured, literate man. It is hard to pin down the influence of that kind of a man. As I said, we became close personal friends and he became a friend to Belsheim the same way. We both just worshiped the man and he knew it.

So Holdsworth wrote to Yale. Charlie Clark wrote back that they did not take young men sight unseen but he would give me a fat fellowship and if I was as good as Holdsworth thought I was then he might give me a job at a later stage. I came to Yale Law School at the beginning of the American Legal Realist movement and I thought they were all crazy. (I fought them in the classroom up and down.)

At Yale I specialized in what were called Credit Transactions and Debtors Estates, two courses that a man named Wesley Sturges taught. Sturges, I think, was the best teacher I ever had. I fought him bitterly all year and woke one spring morning and decided he was right. When he called on me in class that morning he could not believe his ears. I gave him the correct answer and he worked on me for a while and finally decided that I would be a protege of his. He is the man who got me the job at Illinois and like many proteges I went from bitter fighting with him to perhaps too strong an approval. I taught his books for several years, indeed I made my living out of his books for several years. I taught his books at the University of Chicago that summer.

Sturges was the best teacher I ever had, I think the best teacher Yale Law School ever had. He taught many famous people. I would go in and hear him take apart some of the great lawyers from Washington. He would make them switch completely around. There was a man named Steinberg in the class at the time, the number one man in the class. As the students were coming out of the lecture one day I asked him why they let Sturges handle them that way, why they allowed him to change their opinions around. Steinberg said that none of the students could understand why, that Sturges was just too good for them. Sturges was a brilliant man, though he himself was a C student from Columbia, believe it or not.

MACDONALD: And then you were in Illinois for a couple of years?

McDougal: I was there for three years and then came on to Yale. They had told me at Yale that they would invite me back to New Haven in about three years if I turned out to be as good as Holdsworth thought I was.

I loved Illinois. I almost transferred my citizenship from Mississippi to Illinois. And you can understand that that is a pretty hard thing for a Mississippian to do. But I loved it there. I was associate dean at Illinois at the end of the three years.

I was up in Michigan on a fishing trip with some friends and went into a grocery store to get some food. There was a telegram there two weeks old inviting me back to Yale. I took it down to Illinois with me when we went back to Urbana and I went in to see the dean. I was associate dean at that time and I told the dean I did not think I wanted to go back to Yale anymore; I had grown to like the Midwest and wanted to live there. The dean said nothing for quite a long time; he kept looking at the telegram, turning it over and over and over again, very slowly; finally, he looked up at me and said, "Mac, I waited forty years for this but it never came. I would advise you to go."

Macdonald: A gem of a story.

Macdonald: It's now July 1, 1934 and you are now starting out as an associate professor at Yale Law School, soon to be working with Harold Lasswell? When and how did you two meet?

McDougal: I met Harold Lasswell by accident one summer at the University of Chicago. I was invited out to the University of Chicago to teach in the summer of 1935, I think it was, and I lived in a university house right on the campus, in the apartment of one of the professors. I was reading *The New York Times* that morning and saw a review of Lasswell's book, *World Politics and Personal Insecurity,* which is his greatest book. The reviewer, John Chamberlain, said that this was a great book even if I can't understand it but there must be people who can.

Well, at Chicago their practice is to put the name of the instructor on the door while he is lecturing. When I went in to teach my class I looked across the hall and saw the name of Lasswell on the door just across the hall from where I was teaching. I finished up in about an hour and there were noises still coming out of the room across the hall. I thought, "Well, I'll go in and see if I can understand the great man." I went in and sat down and listened to him talk; he was using psychoanalytical techniques to discuss H.G. Wells, whose book everybody in the book clubs was reading that summer. I was reading the book myself. After hearing Lasswell for forty minutes I never bothered finishing it; I felt that I knew what made Wells tick, which I did.

I went up after the class and shook Lasswell's hand and said I hoped he had not minded my dropping in at the back of his class, I was a visiting professor in the law school. He said, "Would you like to have lunch?" I said, "Of course I would love to have lunch." So we walked across the campus to the faculty club where everybody goes to eat and Lasswell and I spent three or four hours talking and I did not find him difficult to understand at all.

I went back to the law school and told them I had met this wonderful man and why didn't they get him on the faculty. They just roared with laughter. They had undertaken a study with him on the Town Hall or something, and the first thing he wanted to know, they said, was whether the place was wired for direct or alternating current; they thought that was very funny and just roared with laughter. This set me back a little.

In those days my wife would entertain so I went back to this lovely apartment we had there on the campus and told her that I wanted to give a dinner party. So we gave a dinner party and invited Lasswell and the law faculty. After dinner was over I rolled out a few bottles and in fifteen minutes I knew who was crazy. Lasswell was just running circles around them and they did not even know what was being done to them. Max Rhinestein was the big poohbah on the Chicago faculty. He was a great man as a scholar but a bit of a dope and no wonder he could not understand Lasswell.

————

MACDONALD: Your collaborative working relationship with Harold Lasswell was unprecedented in modern legal scholarship. We've had Darwin and Huxley in England and Deleuz and Guattari in France but in international law there is nothing to compare to the two cerebral Siamese twins McDougal and Lasswell. You complemented one another.

McDOUGAL: Well, I expected that. When I first met him in Chicago he didn't seem to me to be at all strange. I understood him and I told him that if he came to New York to come on up to Yale and we'd make some connection for him. He turned out not to be a success, which was a surprise. He was not successful in public relations and he called me up one day and said he'd like to come up and talk with me. I told him to come on and by that time I was a power at Yale; at the end of the Second World War we had only seven members of faculty. I got him elected to the faculty and along the way I compromised; I would vote for Emerson and the rest of them would vote for Lasswell so we got him on the faculty. Again it was lucky, you see; the faculty had got so small that I could control it and so it worked out very well for him and for me.

We never talked personal things, it was always business, ideas. Lasswell was wonderful on ideas. I made it clear to the students then and I make it clear to them now that the basic ideas of the law, science and policy stuff all came from Lasswell. I didn't create those ideas but I was able to understand them and use them. That was the contribution I thought I made. And I want to tell you that Lasswell thanked me just before his death; he called me into his room and said he wanted to thank me for all I'd done for him and I told him I'd always thought the shoe was on the other foot. He said, no, that I had done a great deal for him, and I suppose in a sense I did. I made him put his feet on the ground and I rationalized his arguments in a way that he might not otherwise have done.

MACDONALD: What is the story of your famous book on the law of property, McDougal and Haber?

McDOUGAL: Well, the final chapters were on land use planning, community planning, and the book was suppressed. In two states it was alleged that the publication of the book was unlawful, that it violated the Constitution. It was crazy. The book was banned in the state of Texas and the boys down there quit teaching it. They tried to ban it in the state of Washington, but the boys teaching it there said, "The hell with you, I'm going to teach what I want to," and they decided to let him alone, so he continued to teach it in Washington while it was banned in Texas. I had a lot of trouble with that book, people regarded it as a radical book. I supported the notion of planning in the United States and people didn't like that.

MACDONALD: That episode should not be forgotten. Has it been written up? McDougal and Haber is a fine book. I used it when I taught land law in Toronto in the 1950s and '60s. Nobody up there thought the final chapters were radical.

MACDONALD: A different subject now. Of your many books and articles which are your favorites? Which are the ones you most enjoyed doing and that you feel best about?

McDOUGAL: The book on *Law, Science and Policy* reflects the lectures that Lasswell and I gave together over the forty-one-year period that we worked together. I suppose it is the best summary of our basic ideas. I would like to be sure that everybody knows that Lasswell was the real creator of this approach. I want it to be known that Lasswell was largely responsible for the LS&P approach and that the first thirty-five pages are a summary of what he stood for.

Peter Stern was one of my best students and we were going to do a book together on the law of war but he decided that he wanted to practice law for a year or two. Then Feliciano came along. He was already an expert on war. He had been involved in the Philippine War, and he took over and finished up the book that Peter Stern and I were going to do together.

Peter is one of my best friends; he has been one of my greatest supporters throughout my life. He provided the money for the book that I suppose I should be most proud of, the human rights book. Peter Stern put up $200,000 for Chen to work on the human rights book as long as it took to produce it. It took us nearly ten years to finish that book and I enjoyed it. Once I got interested in the subject I probably put more intellectual energy into the topic and came to like it better than any of the subjects I worked with. The human rights field is a wonderful field to work in and I did become deeply involved in that book.

MACDONALD: You have had a charmed life and I've often wondered if there was anything you wanted that didn't come your way or anything you would like to have done but didn't manage to get done.

MCDOUGAL: Oh yes. I tried to go to the International Court of Justice. I tried for the International Court at least three times and was always beaten by a Harvard man. The Harvard people had a better mafia than the Yale people had. I have three former students on the Court right now but I never could make one of the fifteen myself. That's been the principal disappointment of my life.

MACDONALD: You were always a bear for work. Did you ever take any extended holidays?

MCDOUGAL: Not that I know of.

MACDONALD: You are coming up to the "Big Nine-O." Has retirement been good to you? Were there special projects you were reserving for retirement?

MCDOUGAL: I don't regard myself as being retired.

MACDONALD: Thank you for today, for your friendship over the years, and for the inspiration you gave so many of my generation.

REMEMBRANCES

*The following pages comprise excerpts
from letters, essays, and other remembrances
of Myres Smith McDougal from over one hundred
of his many students, colleagues, and friends
around the world.*

A. DALLAS ALBRITTON, '56
Albritton & Associates, Tampa, Florida

For some reason, Mac and I hit it off, perhaps because we were both from the South, a not very popular place in the '50s. At some point I was asked to write an article about him for the *Yale Law Report*. This necessitated many enjoyable conversations, getting to know him, hearing him tell about his youth, his early ambitions, and so on. Early on he was quite interested in politics and said he had thought of running for Congress or the Senate someday but got sidetracked into scholarship.

He was a great teacher and a great scholar, whose range of learning was prodigious. But more than that, Professor McDougal was a great person, and his kindness and concern are legendary.

LAYMAN E. ALLEN, '56

In everyone's life-time there is somebody there in the fork in the road when a significant choice is made.

Mac's openness to new ideas has been my lasting memory of him. He typified for me the Yale Law School.

HARRY H. ALMOND
Professor, National Defense University,
Department of Defense, Washington, D.C. (Retired)

When my character was dangerously attacked in Washington politics, in the context of the SALT negotiations, Mac teamed up with Michael Reisman and ignited an unbelievable coup of support in their important letter to *The New York Times*. Reading that letter in the *Times* lighted a golden glow that will last for me forever.

Myres Smith McDougal

MOHAMMED A. ALMULHIM, '65 LL.M., '70 J.S.D.
Minister of State of the Kingdom of Saudi Arabia

As a world class institution, Yale Law School is the host to many first-class scholars and educators. However, Myres Smith McDougal, a pioneering, ground-breaking leader of legal scholarship, had a major share in this institution's renown beyond American borders. Without Myres Smith McDougal, this institution would not be the same.

Mac is a popular name, and Myres Smith McDougal liked and loved very much that his colleagues and students should call him "Mac" whenever they desired to speak to him.

As a human being, Mac was friendly, considerate, gentle, and appreciative. He had a great sense of humor and a good heart; he loved his students, foreign and national alike, and was extremely eager to help them with all the means available to him.

As an academician, Mac was a great, omni-competent teacher in his classroom. He dispersed knowledge tirelessly, and did not mind repeating his thoughts and explanations in getting his ideas across, and more than occasionally using his humor as a means of persuasion in holding his students' attention.

As an American, Mac was a deep scholar in the eyes of all non-Americans who knew him well. Mac, in fact, symbolized the true image of America in his dignified, courtly demeanor, in his openness, loyalty, honesty, and warm feelings. He was, to say the least, larger than life.

When he joined the Yale Law School faculty and became the chairman of the Graduate Program, Mac strived from the very beginning to make Yale Law School available to potential applicants world wide. He encouraged foreign students, regardless of their nationalities, race, religion, color, or loyalties, to attend Yale Law School. Most of such students after studying went on to become leaders, judges, and law teachers in their respective countries, having been endowed with Yale values and excellence.

Mac's accomplishments are too numerous to outline here, but his legal imprint is most visible in the legacy of the cherished establishment known as "The New Haven School of Jurisprudence." His inclusive-exclusive precise eight values namely, power, well-being, wealth, skill, respect, enlightenment, affection, and rectitude, have been engraved in the memories of his devoted students.

Based upon these values, Mac was the first among his associates to initiate, make and strongly advocate through his writings, the International Law of Human Dignity.

Mac's devoted students, including me, will never forget the question "What does the term international law of human dignity mean?" Mac defined the term as follows: "By an international law of human dignity, I mean the processes of authoritative decision of a world public order in which values are shaped and shared more by persuasion than coercion, and which seeks to promote the greatest production and widest possible sharing, without discrimination irrelevant to merit, of all values among all human beings."[1]

The notion of "international law of human dignity" had evolved and developed in Mac's mind, legally and politically so to speak, as a result of the aftermath of the Second World War. However, Mac, after six decades was more than happy to witness in his lifetime that his genuine thoughts, taught within Yale Law School classrooms about the law of human dignity, had been already materialized through the total collapse of the Soviet Union.

Even though Mac is no longer living among us to advise and teach, his legacy carries on not only in his small island which is Yale Law School, but in all places around the world where Mac's ideals are being advocated and enhanced.

On a personal level, I would like to show my sincere gratitude to my beloved teacher Myres Smith McDougal, for exposing me to deep scholarship and in widening my horizon to legal knowledge and proper methods of research.

As devoted friends from Saudi Arabia, my wife Naeemah Alqadhi and I feel his loss and are grieved by his absence.

MORGAN AMES, '47

He was the most brilliant person I ever knew!

ATILLA DE SOUZA LEÃO ANDRADE, JR., '72 LL.M., '77 MSL
São Paulo, Brazil

He was certainly the most impressive scholar and human being I have met in the USA. We will all miss Professor McDougal but he shall always be present in our hearts and minds.

WILLIAM ASCHER

I will always hold Mac in the highest level of admiration.

---

[1] See McDougal & Associates, Studies in World Public Order, 987 (Yale Univ. Press, 1960).

MATTEO BARADA, '65 LL.M.
General Manager, Ministry of Merchant Marine, Rome, Italy

Power, wealth, skill, enlightenment ... how may one forget the teachings of Professor Myres S. McDougal and those of Professor Harold Lasswell? He is living and will live in everyone of his students as far as his teachings will stay deeply rooted in their minds.

Professor Myres. S. McDougal was a leading figure, a unique man and an incomparable teacher.

LEO D. BARRY, '68 LL.M.
Justice, Supreme Court of Newfoundland

Myres McDougal in 1967 recommended me for a fellowship to study at Yale. He was an inspiring teacher of international law. Even more importantly, he showed how one could be intellectually rigorous, yet personally very kind.

In 1970 I had the opportunity to have him come to Newfoundland for a Learned Societies Conference. My wife and I spent several happy days with him. Later in the 1970s he aided me in work with the Government of Newfoundland by providing an opinion on ownership of offshore oil and gas. This past year we saw the first oil field developed, with great benefits for our Province. I owe a great debt to Myres McDougal. To repay it, all I can do is try and pass on in some small way to others the benefit of what I learned from a wonderful teacher and marvelous human being.

HELEN I. BENDIX, '76
Judge, Los Angeles Municipal Court

He was a wonderful teacher and the world is diminished by his death. He taught me a new way to look at the law and to understand the importance of a society governed by laws.

Remembrances

MAHESH BIJAWAT, '61 LL.M., '63 J.S.D.
Professor, Banaras Hindu University, Varanasi, India

It is seldom that you meet a person during your lifetime, whom you not only admire but who leaves an indelible impression upon you. Such a person was the late Professor Myres McDougal. A colossus in the academic field, his aptitude for research and writing was difficult to match. I met him for the first time in my home town of Varanasi (India) in February 1960. At that time I was an assistant professor of law at Banaras Hindu University and had applied for admission to the Graduate Program at Yale Law School. I was accepted and reached New Haven in September 1960.

There were over fifty students in the graduate program from nearly twenty countries and it was truly an international gathering. Professor McDougal's aim was to spread the name of the Yale Law School all over the world and so he admitted students from as many countries as possible for the LL.M. course. Most of them went back after completing the course and occupied high positions of authority in their respective countries and made Yale known there. There were many students from India in the program when I joined. Professor McDougal was my mentor, guide, and guardian throughout my three years' stay at the Yale Law School. Some of the foreign students felt homesick and frustrated initially, and Professor McDougal proved to be a pillar of strength to them.

He wanted all foreign students to take his course on "Law, Science, and Policy," which he taught in "McDougalian" language, which was difficult to grasp and understand. I was one of the few who did not take this course, but he never held that against me. I was accepted for the J.S.D program in September 1961.

Professor McDougal visited my wife and myself at our residence. He was always anxious to know about my progress and welfare. When I completed my J.S.D. and left for India in April 1963, he gave me his blessings and good wishes. I kept in touch with him through Christmas greetings. I came to Harvard Law School during 1971–72 to pursue the International Tax Program, and I made it a point to see him at Yale. He was, as usual, busy with writing a new book, using a magnifying glass to read. When my wife and myself came again in 1988, he had retired and shifted to a small room in the Law School. The whole room was full of books and notes and there was hardly any place to sit. The last time we met him was in 1995 when he was in a nursing home. He recognized us though his eyesight was failing and inquired about us and other Indian students who had graduated from the Law School.

When I received information this year that Professor McDougal had finally left for his heavenly abode in May, it grieved us very much. Here was a man, who besides being a brilliant academician, was humane, humble, and generous. Someone has said, "Men may come and men may go, but I go on forever." To this I would add, "And some men leave their footprints on the sand of time." Professor Myres S. McDougal was one such man.

OSCAR BLAYTON, '77

For myself, and those who could not be here, the words regarding the quality of life and human dignity will always ring clearly.

FRANCIS A. BOYLE
Professor, University of Illinois, College of Law, Champaign, Illinois

I first met Mac when I was in law school. Dick Baxter brought him into class around 1974 to lecture against the War Powers Resolution, arguing that it was a terrible infringement on the president's power. Of course, I disagreed, pointing out that Nixon had just invaded Cambodia and had gotten away with it. If anything, we needed more restraints on the imperial president, not fewer. Mac and I argued for the entire class session, back and forth. At the end of class Mac said: "Well I don't believe I have convinced the gentleman sitting in the front row, but I am sure I have convinced the rest of you that the War Powers Resolution is unconstitutional." Mac always liked a good argument. We would have several over the years. But I always had the greatest respect for his opinion.

May Mac rest in peace.

GERALDO BRINDEIRO, '82 LL.M., '90 J.S.D.
Attorney General of Brazil

His death is a loss not only for the community of the Yale Law School, but also gives a sense of profound bereavement to me, who will long remember the profound influence of his thought and his many kindnesses towards me.

MARGARET BRUSASCO-MACKENZIE, '61 LL.M.
Directorate-General, Environment, European Commission, Brussels, Belgium

When I was participating in the LL.M. Programme in 1960/61, I had the great pleasure of studying several courses with Professor McDougal. I was also privileged to work very closely with him and to contribute to one of his many books. Coming straight from an English Law School, (King's College) London, which had given me an excellent but mainly black-letter law legal training, it was a revelation to enter Professor McDougal's classes. He has left me with an abiding interest in public international law, and a far loftier concept of legal education, and what the profession should be. His inspiration and his teaching has also been most useful to me, both in a career as a law teacher and, especially as a negotiator of international treaties in the field of the environment, on behalf of the European Commission.

Apart from the professional legacy, I have an abiding memory of a Southern gentleman whose courtesy, warmth and grace of character shone through on all occasions.

KARIN M. BURKE, '81
New York Law School

I was fortunate to have met Professor Myres S. McDougal as a young law student in his Jurisprudence class at New York Law School, and was quickly inspired by his policy science approach to law. Our friendship continued over the years even after my graduation. He was a wonderful teacher, mentor, and friend, and a great influence on my career and my approach to law. I fondly recall the gentle cadence of his Mississippi accent, his hearty laugh, and colorful expressions ("how do we get off this squirrel cage?").

He was the epitome of what a great "teacher" should be—he inspired, challenged, and affirmed each of his students, and always treated all with dignity, respect, and value. He truly practiced the goal of "human dignity." Indeed, if there is one quality that stands out in my mind about him, it would not be his brilliance, creativity, or scholarly preeminence (although he certainly possessed all of these) but that he treated each person with dignity—as though you were a person of worth and value *to him*. As great and busy and important as he was, he always made time for us, his students, genuinely seemed to enjoy our company, and conveyed that what we had to say was important to him. This quality, so rare and yet so genuine on his part, meant so much to me as a young law student and later, as a new lawyer just starting out on my legal career.

He was unfailingly kind and generous. One of the ways I observed this was in his helping young people launch their careers, offering his personal contacts, wise counsel, and the strength of his recommendation. There was nothing of "self" that he held in reserve if he was able to help one of his students. It was rather typical that he would look for ways to help others shine. In one of his classes, for example, my colleague, Deborah DeLeo, and I researched and wrote a paper as a final examination. Much to my surprise and delight, Mac suggested that the paper was good enough to be published, and helped arrange for the eventual publication of our article in a Yale journal.

Professor McDougal influenced so many people positively in his lifetime— probably more so than he could possibly have imagined. It is said that he was not "formally" religious, but in his treatment of others I believe he truly lived out the gospel message, love of his fellow man, much better than most. He was a great man, and I will miss him very much.

JOSÉ A. CABRANES, '65
Judge, U.S. Court of Appeals, Second Circuit, New Haven, Connecticut

Myres McDougal is gone. His family, his friends, his colleagues, and his students are joined together in mourning his death.

I am here as one of Mac's students, as an admirer of his contributions to the life of the law, and as a beneficiary of his friendship for the past thirty-six years.

I arrived at Yale Law School in the early 1960s, at the height of Mac's powers as a scholar and as a baron of the Law School faculty. The McDougal I met in 1962 was devoted to theory, but he was no mere theoretician; he was a person of size in the proverbial "real world."

Mac's scholarship and his advocacy had touched most of the great foreign policy debates of the 1940s, 1950s, and 1960s: United States participation in the new, post-war order; the principles of law governing the exercise of coercive authority by great powers in that new order; the international protection of human rights (a subject that Mac helped to place on the map, and which he introduced to law school curricula); the use of executive agreements in the conduct of our foreign affairs; the application of international law by the United States tribunals; the law of the sea; and the law of outer space (an interest of his that some of us in 1962 regarded, quite incorrectly, as eccentric).

With theory or without theory, Myres McDougal was, without a doubt, the greatest international lawyer of his time.

Not to be forgotten in all of this was the quiet and significant work of this Mississippian in domestic affairs—notably, in the transformation of his state and region. Always a hero at home and at his alma mater, Ole Miss, McDougal helped to reshape legal education there—and thereby helped to reshape the public life of that state. He did this by his sustained efforts to bring some of its best alumni to do graduate work at Yale and by placing Yale Law School grad-

---

Judge Cabranes' remarks were given at the gathering in the Yale Law School Dean's Office following Professor McDougal's interment in Grove Street Cemetery, New Haven, Connecticut

uates, Mississippians and non-Mississippians alike, on its law faculty. I well recall how amazed I was to learn, in the mid-1960s, that virtually every member (perhaps *every* member) of the Ole Miss Law School faculty, including its dean, was a graduate of Yale Law School. [As the Marxists used to say, "I ask you, Comrade, was this a mere coincidence?"]

In all of these important affairs, Mac deployed what Dean Eugene V. Rostow famously described as the "three McDougals"—the first was described by Rostow as "Senator McDougal;" the second McDougal, according to Rostow, was the friend and teacher, and the third McDougal was the scholar and theorist.

Since no one has written better on the subject of Senator McDougal, let me quote a fragment of Dean Rostow's great essay on Mac, written in the *Yale Law Journal* on the occasion of Mac's assumption of emeritus status in 1975.

> Myres McDougal is not a complex personality, as many students of the subject have supposed. Scholars in the field, writers of theses and learned monographs, have created a mystery where there is none. Confused by Mac's diversity, they have missed the key point because it is too simple for their solemn methods: [He] is not one man, but three remarkable men contained in one man's skin.
>
> The first of the three McDougals—perhaps we should identify him as Senator McDougal—is a consummate Mississippi politician of the old school: worldly, perceptive, and persuasive—principled, to be sure, but above all an artist in power. There is not a trace of Senator Claghorn in Senator McDougal—no bombast, nothing of the demagogue. But he knows about power, gathers it, cultivates it, and uses it, with a grace Senator Richard Russell and Mr. Sam Rayburn would have understood and appreciated.... Above all, he is the spider at the center of a worldwide Old Boy network which is the marvel of the age. It deals with the very stuff of power: appointments, promotions, honors, the make-up of key committees, assistance to a brother or a sister in difficulty for the moment. A sabbatical, let us say, in Bangkok? The deanship, hypothetically, at Freiburg or Florida or Cornell? A grant and a visiting appointment to tide over a period of political turbulence at home? [*JAC aside:* Lord knows how many of Mac's students in the Third World were placed out of harm's way by virtue of a visiting appointment at an American university, or by an appointment to the international civil service, facilitated by Mac.] Nomination to the staff or even higher reaches of a federal government? Nothing could be simpler. Nor could any set of decisionmaking processes be managed with greater elegance or discretion.
>
> Mac has never given Senator McDougal his head, of course.... The other McDougals have required too much even of Mac's titanic energies to allow the Senator domination in his life.

As a result of the work of the three "McDougals," separately and jointly, the Yale Law School—already the country's greatest national law school—became the American law school of greatest renown in the world beyond our borders. When I studied at Cambridge, England, in the mid-1960s, and when I was involved later in numerous international activities, it was clear to me that the international renown of the Yale Law School was primarily based on the work and influence of Myres Smith McDougal.

At this sad moment, I recall all of this—I recall my teacher and my friend, Myres McDougal—with affection, admiration and profound respect.

The medieval Spanish poet Jorge Manrique captured my view, at the end of his meditation on the death of his father, in a Spanish that is as simple and beautiful as it is archaic and (perhaps) untranslatable:

> *Y aunque la vida murió*
> *nos dexó harto consuelo su memoria*

"And although his life [has] died, we are greatly consoled by our remembrance of him"—or, in the more liberal translation by Longfellow—

> *[His] light shall linger round us yet,*
> *Bright, radiant and blest.*

THOMAS D. CLARK
Professor Emeritus, University of Kentucky, College of Law, Lexington, Kentucky

In 1925, Myres was editor of the *Mississippian*, the University of Mississippi student newspaper, and I was a reporter. That year Myres was chosen a Rhodes Scholar, and our paths separated. In later years we renewed our association and friendship.

As a student at Ole Miss, Myres was a bright student who came out of the northeast Mississippi hills with a grim determination to succeed, and succeed he did. I personally have taken great pride in his accomplishments.

CYNTHIA PRICE COHEN

I am one of a group of students who might never have been exposed to the intellect and personality of Professor McDougal, had he not been forced to retire from Yale Law School.

Fortunately for me, the assistant dean of New York Law School (Margaret Bearn)—knowing of my interest in children's rights—recommended that I enroll in Professor McDougal's seminar on "Human Rights and World Public Order." As was typical of Mac, he took all of us seminar students under his wing.

Although I was unable to convince Mac to put children's rights into his human rights book, he consistently and continuously encouraged my interests in the topic. A few years later—when I published my first journal article on the Convention on the Rights of the Child—it was Mac who provided the title: "The Human Rights of Children."

There is no doubt that meeting and knowing Professor McDougal changed my life!

LORI FISLER DAMROSCH, '76

How much I have absorbed beginning twenty-five years ago here and which has influenced me ever since.

CHERYL A. DeFILIPPO
Former Assistant to Myres S. McDougal

Throughout the fifteen years I worked with Mac, he was a constant source of inspiration, support and wisdom. Our friendship extended beyond work and I was fortunate to accompany him to many social events, including a trip to Mississippi, where he was honored with a Lifetime Achievement Award, and watching the Superbowl at Evergreen Woods. I would tell Mac which team had the ball and he would then explain the plays to me. It was a fun way for me to learn the game, and to spend time with such a multifaceted person.

When Mac congratulated me on becoming an attorney, he gave me the following words of advice: "Cheryl," he said, "have fun, work hard and stand on a high box." I cherish this last bit of advice and am very grateful for having had the opportunity to know and learn from such a wonderful and generous person.

FRANCIS M. DENG, '65 LL.M., '68 J.S.D.
Senior Fellow, The Brookings Institution, Washington, D.C.

For me personally, Mac and Harold Lasswell had a profound impact on my intellectual and moral outlook. Although I cannot claim to have mastered the discipline of their Law, Science, and Policy theory, or to be their disciple in that sense, their framework provided me with intellectual tools that have guided me ever since. Before coming to Yale, words like "human dignity" and "values" were notions of moral judgements to be avoided in legal thought. Law, Science, and Policy gave these words an empirical and analytical meaning that made them indispensable to understanding political, social, and legal processes.

I now wonder how anyone can make policy judgements without human dignity or value categories as essential terms of reference. I have been struck by the extent to which these concepts have influenced the professional language and outlook of Mac's former students, whether they are academics, judges, lawyers, diplomats, or politicians. And Mac's former students from the Sudan are indeed actively participating in all these fields.

Just as enduring as his intellectual impact was his concern for the personal welfare and development of his students. For me, one of the last personal touches from Mac was a gift of his and Lasswell's two volumes of *Jurisprudence for a Free Society,* with a very thoughtful and moving inscription. Within a month of my receiving this precious gift, Mac went into a nursing home. Even at that late hour, I received from him a letter which still glowed with magnanimity and grace.

Whatever our faith and belief in the life hereafter, a vital aspect of the continuation of identity and influence after life as we know it in this world is what we have done, the people we have touched, and the influence the legacy of our life will continue to have among the living.

Mac was a good man and in all religions, goodness defies death and ensures a place in everlasting life. But even in my more modest definition of immorality, very few could be assured of enduring memory among so many as McDougal. His intellectual might, moral vision, human compassion, and inspiring leadership will always endear him to those of us who were privileged enough to know him.

On behalf of myself and my Sudanese compatriots who were Mac's students, I feel honored and privileged to share these personal reflections about a man who was our teacher, our leader, and our friend. May his soul enjoy peace, dignity, and freedom, ideals to which he dedicated his life in this world.

ALAN C. DREWSEN, '73
Corporate Vice-President & General Counsel,
Empire Blue Cross/Blue Shield, New York, New York

Myres McDougal lived a long and productive life, filled with the professional accomplishment and personal decency that earned the deep respect of his colleagues and the awed admiration of generations of students.

KRESZENTIA J. DUER, '74

It's impossible to fully express my gratitude and deep affection for my great friend and mentor, Mac. How terribly he will be missed.

E. DONALD ELLIOTT, '74
Professor (Adjunct) of Law, Yale Law School

In memory of a great and kindly man—and one whose friendship and encouragement helped me a great deal.

CARL M. FRANKLIN, '56 J.S.D.
Vice-President Emeritus and Professor of Law,
University of Southern California, Los Angeles, California

We have lost a great and good friend in Mac.

BERNARD GARTLIR, '41 LL.B.
Partner, Hofheimer, Gartlir & Gross, New York, New York

I was a student of Myres McDougal in his famous Real Property course and remember him fondly as an inspiring and dedicated teacher.

I also personally remember him as the professor who interviewed me at the time of my application for admission to the Law School. That experience was most exhilarating and was my first exposure to his sharp wit and extraordinary intuitive knowledge. The Law School was indeed honored by his talents. He represented the finest traditions of teaching.

GEORGE E. GLOS, '59 LL.M., '60 J.S.D.
Falls Church, Virginia

Thanks to Professor McDougal, my stay at the Law School was very productive and enjoyable. Professor McDougal was a great teacher and friend and I continued in contact with him until his death. I also came to New Haven for the celebration of his eightieth birthday.

Myres Smith McDougal

STEPHEN GOROVE, '50 LL.M., '52 J.S.D.
Professor Emeritus of Law, University of Mississippi

Myres S. McDougal was one of my former law professors at Yale, whose supe-rior intellect and warm friendship I had the privilege of enjoying over a span of almost five decades.

In light of what may be called a tenet of the social process in a nutshell, *i.e.,* 'people seeking values through institutions on resources,' he developed with his colleague, Harold D. Lasswell, an eminent social scientist, new insights into the understanding of the world political process of authoritative decision mak-ing. He continued to expand its ramifications further, with varied other associ-ates, in a series of brilliant scholarly treatises dealing with crucial issues of world public order relating to the oceans, outer space, and human rights, within the broad framework of what he called "Jurisprudence For a Free Society."

Myres McDougal was not just another world authority but a giant among giants, a shining beacon pointing the way toward hitherto uncharted waters. He carried the intellectual fight for acceptance of what many regarded in the forties as a revolutionary scholarly endeavor, especially when viewed through the prism of Austinian tradition and the almost ironclad logic of Hans Kelsen's pure theory of law. In collaboration with his associates, several of them his for-mer students, he applied his emerging policy-oriented jurisprudence to vital contemporary problems of world public order by making use of the findings of modern physical and social science. His work aimed to offer a framework for decisions, a system not only to enhance the minimum world public order but perhaps to attain an optimum public order that would be based upon and would grant the highest recognition to the dignity of man. His writings, which reflect a comprehensive survey of the world decision making process, rank among the finest original contributions to international legal scholarship.

As a member of the prestigious *Institut de Droit International* and, at times, president of many leading domestic and international associations, he was the recipient of innumerable honors and distinctions. One recent honor which he cherished with sincere affection was a Lifetime Achievement Award from his undergraduate alma mater, the University of Mississippi, the very institution at which he had also served as a teaching fellow in the mid-twenties.

Mac, as he was affectionately known by many, always had time to see his students, lend them a helping hand and provide much needed guidance and advice. On appropriate occasions, he did this with a twinkle in his eyes accom-panied by a witty remark. His warm human qualities and profound respect for human dignity were deeply embedded in his innate character and personality and were ever present notwithstanding his relentless intellectual advocacy and defense of his school of thought. His presence, acumen, true friendship, and humor will be sorely missed by international legal scholars and jurisprudential thinkers all over the world.

KARL B. GRAF, '48 LL.M.
Rogue Bluffs, Maine

I would have liked him to know how truly I appreciated him and how grateful I was and the impact he had on my life.

VIRGINIA M. GRANDISON

Mac was a special teacher who will be truly missed.

W. GEORGE GRANDISON, '72

Mac was a very special part of our lives at the Law School and an inspiration as a scholar and a friend.

CARL J. GREEN, '65
Deputy Senior Representative, Hitachi, Ltd., Washington, D.C.

I have fond memories of a wonderful teacher, mentor, and human being. I feel quite privileged to have been his student.

WILLIAM S. GREEN, '52 LL.B.
Retired Partner, Reed, Smith, Shaw & McClay, Washington, D.C.

Myres McDougal was a giant among the Law School faculty of his time. I will never forget him.

LUKE CHARLES HARRIS, '77 J.D., '80 LL.M.

To a wonderful man of enormous grace who epitomized the human dignity we aspire to for the world.

IBNE HASSAN
New York, New York

Professor Myres S. McDougal was a very special person and intellectual, who brought knowledge and happiness to the lives of many people. He was always ready to guide, help, and inspire by his ways, which were simple, sincere and deep. The impressions he has left have touched lives of innumerable persons around the globe. His memories shall always remain alive and will continue to enlighten many of his students, associates and colleagues.

He is gone, but he will always be a beacon to my life, as for many others. I will always cherish his blissful friendship, association and advice.

May God bless him.

PARVEZ HASSAN, '63 LL.M.
Hassan & Hassan (Advocates), Lahore, Pakistan

He was like a mountain in the field of environmental law and I have repeatedly said, even publicly, that after my parents no individual has influenced my life as did Professor McDougal.

A. ANDREW HAUK, '42 J.S.D.
Senior Judge and Chief Judge Emeritus, U.S. District Court,
Central District of California, Los Angeles, California

I was in residence at Yale Law (1938–39) in pursuit of a J.S.D. degree I received in 1942. Needless to say, my encounter with Mac when I started that year of residence was somewhat disconcerting as I had just finished three years of law school at Catholic University, where I was rather completely immersed in Scholastic logic and was therefore, a "Thomist" in legal philosophy. But Mac initiated me into this newly created jurisprudence with such gentleness and understanding that it became part of my own philosophical approach to law which I have gratefully utilized on the Bench. For the entire succeeding year, Mac always made himself available to each one of us in graduate school for his helpful direction and suggestions.

So I say, God bless him and grant him eternal rest. We salute him with the words of the Roman solider, AVE ATQUE VALE.

THOMAS, E. HEADRICK, '60
Provost, University at Buffalo, State University of New York, Buffalo, New York

I am reminded of the good fortune I and others had to have known, learned from and been inspired by him. He truly was a great man whose influence and ideals live on.

LOUIS, J. HECTOR, '41
Chairman, Lucille P. Markey Charitable Trust, Miami, Florida

Mac arrived at the Yale Law School fresh from a British legal education a few years before I did the same. I'm told he left England with the same conviction I had, that the law is some sort of brooding omnipresence in the skies which we can articulate clearly if we just work at it hard enough, and then made one of the great St. Paul-like conversions to the functional approach and "running it both ways." He took delight in dousing me with the same bath of cold water when I arrived, and we developed the sort of friendship that grows between two converts.

GEOFFREY E. HEGGS, '54 LL.M.
London, United Kingdom

He will be remembered with affection by many generations of students. The one lesson which I learned from Mac was never to consider an issue superficially but analyse all the constituent elements and this occasionally produced very gratifying results.

PIETER J. HOETS, '49 LL.M.

On this day, October 4, 1998 at Yale Law School my thoughts return to that day in September 1947, yes fifty-one years ago, that I had the great luck of meeting Mac for the first time here under this very roof. The way he subsequently guided me with his wisdom, care and friendship not only in the classroom, but later in The Hague, was not only a tremendous support for a young Dutch lawyer from Leiden who, after the thunder of World War II sought his way in the world, but also as one example of how Mac has steered generations of lawyers from all corners of the globe to his vision of a better world. He was a giant, but his work will continue.

ANGELA HOLDER, '75 LL.M.

I shall never forget his kindness to a Southerner who came to Yale. I hope I transmit to my students what Mac transmitted to me.

WILLIAM E. HOLDER, '64 LL.M.
Deputy General Counsel, Legal Department,
International Monetary Fund, Washington, D.C.

Mac was the leading intellectual mentor of my life, impacting on my professional career at several critical phases.

GARY N. HORLICK, '73
O'Melveny & Myers, Washington, D.C.

Mac's kindness, courtesy, and hospitality to new law students were legendary. I would also note his wonderfully understated sense of humor, and of enjoyment at the paradoxes of life and law. I arrived at Yale as a first-year law student having just completed a year-long program with Robert Jennings, Derek Bowett *et al.* at Cambridge, and Mac was marvelous at elucidating, without criticism or any negative implication, the difference in approach between Cambridge and the New Haven School (typically modest of Mac).

Finally, as we all know he was always willing to drop whatever he was doing—undoubtedly more important—to listen with sympathy and offer guidance to law students' ideas.

It is hard to imagine Yale Law School without him.

KAREN A. HUDES, '76
Senior Counsel, The World Bank, Washington, D.C.

Myres McDougal, or Mac as he was referred to fondly by his many fans, will be sorely missed. Mac developed a comprehensive approach to legal theory, referred to as "The New Haven School of Jurisprudence," which is considered by some as the most important jurisprudential statement to emerge in the post-war period. Mac collaborated for more than forty years with the famous political scientist Harold Lasswell, who founded communications theory, to come up with a comprehensive legal philosophy based upon the tenet that values and social processes form the cornerstone of legal thought.

Drawing upon psychology, legal experience, and communications theory, McDougal and Lasswell developed a policy-oriented approach which required any legal analysis to begin by examining the underlying values on which this analysis rested. This approach called for great intellectual rigor and honesty, qualities which Mac personified. In an effort to get to the bottom of a matter, Mac's writing style could become opaque at times.

Mac was always accessible to his students, however, and the best way to describe his teaching style was "nurturing." Mac didn't foist his opinions upon his students, but was careful to validate whatever viewpoint that person brought to the classroom, recognizing the value of each person's contribution. What Mac couldn't countenance, however, was pompousness or authority parading as truth. To Mac, law was never an absolute, but an expression or reflection of the values and aspirations of the society that spawned it.

Mac was a southern gentleman. He was traditional and courtly. But the most important qualities which I recall were his enormous warmth and generosity. Whenever you would see him, no matter how often, he would express great glee and genuinely want to know how you were doing. One of his students, Joe Fortenberry, was also from Mississippi, and Joe died at forty. I just had lunch with his widow, who remembered visiting Mac in New Haven some time ago. Well, Mac dropped everything and took her out to lunch. That was Mac.

VICKI HUGSTAD, '85

One of my enduring memories of Mac is the way he good-naturedly challenged us in class on occasions when he'd ask a particularly vexing question to which no one had a response. He'd wait a few moments, look around the room, and choose his foil with a curt "Mr./Miss ___! Let's see how good you *really* are!" I have to admit, I didn't always rise to the occasion, but it inspired me (and I suspect, most of my classmates) to work even harder to meet the high expectations of this professor whom we so admired and respected. Even now, many years later, I often think of his challenging words when faced with a daunting situation—and they still inspire me and bring back fond memories of a wonderful teacher and mentor.

Myres Smith McDougal

JACK P. JEFFERIES, '52 LL.M., '54 J.S.D.
Newport, Rhode Island

I write as a friend of Mac's for forty-seven years.

I first met Mac when I came to Yale Law School at the age of twenty-two to study with Mac for my LL.M. and J.S.D. in international law.

Years later I became a director and then the president of the Policy Science Center, and served as president until the appointment of our present leader, Andy Willard.

Over the forty-seven years, Mac and I met or talked by phone every month or so. He was a personal friend as well as my mentor.

Mac was brilliant, a delightful friend, warm and kind, and always understanding.

He had a great deal of respect for his students and he would "go that extra mile" to help any of them if asked.

I did, on various occasions ask for his help and received it when I was seeking scholarships at Yale, later when I was seeking an army commission in JAG (International Affairs Division) at the Pentagon, when I was looking for a job with a law firm, and during future years when I practiced law at Lord, Day & Lord in New York. Mac was always there when you needed him. His advice was always helpful. In 1958 he tutored me on the law of the sea so I could properly advise my clients.

Mac knowingly and carefully planned and built his world-wide realm of followers and advocates for the cause of Law, Science, and Policy. In the 1950's his Graduate Program brought students from around the world who became friends and advocates of Mac's teaching. In essence, Mac had his own "World University."

Mac was an international law advisor not only to teachers, but also, on numerous occasions, to government leaders, judges, and lawyers.

I will not today catalogue his many academic accomplishments or the many new pathways he carved out in legal thinking. Mac was so far ahead of his time in legal scholarship that the world is still trying to catch up with his thinking.

Mac always sent me autographed copies of his latest publication and when we talked, he would ask what I thought of the material he had published. And then he would discuss his next publication plans for new books and legal articles.

While a graduate student at Yale, I helped Mac research and prepare some of his extensive Hague lectures. It was always a great pleasure working with him.

I will never forget when Mac called me during the Vietnam War (Nixon years) to say "something very important is about to happen to you." He then had me elected as president of the 'Fund for Education in World Order.'

The Fund raised millions of dollars for scholarships in international law and international affairs at Yale, Columbia, and Princeton. The Fund continues today as "The Fund for Peace" in Washington D.C.

Mac had a great sense of humor, which served him well over the years in making thousands of friends and allies.

Harold Lasswell who, as you know wrote continuously, once remarked, "I think Mac works too hard." Mac would say, "Lasswell is a genius." Their friendship was unique. In recent years, Mac always feared God would not provide him with enough time to complete his latest and longest work *Jurisprudence for a Free Society,* and he was so pleased when he finished this work as he had promised Lasswell he would do so if possible.

Of course, Mac's work will continue in Michael Reisman's teachings and the work of the Policy Sciences Center.

We are all so lucky to have known Mac. He was a brilliant scholar and always a true friend.

CHUN PYO JHONG, '58 LL.M., '61 J.S.D.
Kim & Chang, Seoul, Korea

There are many unforgettable experiences and lessons that I gained and learned from Professor McDougal, a great scholar and educator.

DOUGLAS M. JOHNSTON, '59 LL.M., '62 J.S.D.
Professor, National University of Singapore, Faculty of Law, Singapore

I would like to offer a simple tribute from an admiring disciple.

We are twelve time-zones apart, but distance in this case may lend perspective. Although I rarely had the opportunity to return to New Haven after my last sojourn—at the beginning of my "Chinese phase" in 1966—I never felt very far from Mac, and I still find myself responding to the demands he made on our intellect and imagination, when we were young. He shaped my career even more than he could have known.

My first year at Yale (1958–59) was the most important of my life. It was the year I met and married my wife in New Haven! It was also my first experience

---

Professor Johnston's remembrance is submitted with his wife, Judith E. Johnston

of the thrill of intellectual confrontation. Mac was "geared for combat," as he so often felt it necessary to remind us. Simple soldiers of the line, we followed the tank-force of policy science in a great, enthralling, daily assault on the citadel of legal orthodoxy.

Later in life I learned how to articulate what, above all, I had learned at New Haven: that the greatest academic challenge of all is to find a way of combining the traditional U.S. law school quest for excellence-in-rigor with the policy science quest for excellence-in-sophistication. For every profound, close-quarters scrutiny of a complex problem or a fundamental issue, we were taught the merits of a think-plan, a framework for systematic analysis. Even if we are bound to fail to attain total sophistication, the McDougal-Lasswell framework of policy analysis equipped us to engage in comprehensive scholarship, as intelligently as the good Lord has enabled us. No graduate student was ever more richly rewarded.

Over the forty years since I first attended Yale Law School, my career has coincided with two significant juridical events: the revolution in the law of the sea and the emergence of environmentalism. Each is a reflector of what policy science offers to the scholarly community.

Mac was neither a prophet nor an advocate of the diplomatic revolution in the law of the sea. His pre-UNCLOS III preference for inclusive use of the ocean, qualified by acceptance of certain exclusive coastal state authority, was neo-Grotian, far removed from the neo-Seldenian outcome of the diplomatic arena. But none of us in the early 1960's could foresee the outreach, arguably the overreach, of the coastal state's quasi-sovereign prerogative in the regulation and management of coastal seas.

Even more significantly from a policy science perspective, the period of diplomatic transition from UNCLOS I in 1958 to the start-up of UNCLOS III in the late 1960's was also a period of *intellectual* revolution. In 1958 the law of the sea was still essentially a small compartment within the discipline of public international law, consisting of a tightly compacted corpus of legal rules and qualifications framed around the classic distinction between territorial waters and the high seas: between the nearly full sovereignty of the coastal state, on the one hand, and common (world community) right of ocean access and use, on the other. The blackness and whiteness of this famous distinction offended McDougal's sense of reasonableness and his sense of reality. In fisheries, for example, McDougal encouraged his students to explore the potentiality of "modified authority," in the jargon of the day: authority vested in regulatory bodies, or regimes as they came to be called, possessed of management authority conferred by the participating states to exercise controls justified by the best scientific knowledge about the status of the stocks. Within the inclusive neo-Grotian framework, McDougal favored good-faith negotiation by interested and informed states of arrangements designed to preserve the resources and environment of the world's oceans. The key to good ocean management was seen to be the best possible scientific understanding, as the most rational basis for reasonable and consented self-constraint by user-states.

The need for modified authority over the ocean had to be proven through contextual inquiry. Only by scholarly investigation of all the ocean users and claimants and their inter-relationships could the process of decision-making which results in law be clearly identified and justified.

The lasting contribution of Myres McDougal to the law of the sea consists, then, not of his influence on the outcome of the diplomatic arena, but of his influence on the scholarly community of law of the sea specialists who provided the literature of commentary and analysis during the years of political reformulation. Those of us privileged to have a role in the professional commentary and analysis of the UNCLOS III years—the years of the Law of the Sea Institute, especially its Rhode Island phase—were annual witnesses to the broadening out of the law-of-the-sea specialist's mind-set. The annual LSI conferences of that seminal period provided the intellectual energy of *full context inquiry,* characterized by inputs of geographers, economists, political scientists, biologists, ecologists, geologists, and other disciplines. In the multi-disciplinary mode of policy science, the new generation of law of the sea specialists created a field of cross-fertilizing ideas, values, and constructs, guaranteeing that legal issues in ocean use and management could never again be divorced from the real world context of contending factors and considerations. Nowhere else perhaps is the impact of McDougal's corrective range of vision more clearly and more triumphantly established.

But for the accident of history, Mac would surely have devoted a major work to what is now accepted by all as a cognate field of inquiry: a field often described as *international environmental law and policy.* We have only the benefit of a short, overview paper of 1971, published by the New York Academy of Sciences, to sense the range of vision that Mac would have invested in the second great legal evolution, which took place in the years between the initial action planning associated with the 1972 Stockholm Conference on the Human Environment and the comprehensive, full-context, factual inquiries of the 80s and 90s. Here too the McDougal insistence on the weighting of fact and value is seen, through his students and our students, in the multi-disciplinary holistic frameworks of integrated concepts that now characterize the highly sophisticated field of environmental policy analysis and evaluation. The richness and sensitivity of the best and most rational brand of modern environmentalism owes much to the extraordinary open-mindedness inspired by the policy science of McDougal and his great collaborator, Harold Lasswell.

In his later years McDougal regretted displays of excess, irresponsibility, and rigidity in the diplomatic arena. For many of us who have spent our careers in the fields of marine and environmental law and policy, new issues have arisen to challenge our New Haven sense of reasonableness. Many of us, for example, have reacted sharply against the most extreme versions of the so called "precautionary principle," involving a reverse onus of proof that puts impossible demands on the scientific community, reducing the prospect of reasonable constraints and rational management. In the same vein we have protested against the overreaction of the diplomatic community to the supposed menace of the driftnetters' "walls of death." But we do not always agree among ourselves. Some of us oppose anything that falls far short of strict compliance with globally negotiated text, such as the baseline delineation provisions of the 1982 U.N. Convention on the Law of the Sea, while others among us may opt for a greater degree of flexibility in all but the most dangerous cases of deviant state behavior. As a Canadian, I remember with gratitude Mac's defense of the Canadian government's initial resort to measured unilateralism for protection of the ice-covered Arctic Ocean environment. The late Wolfgang Friedmann, his respected adversary on that memorable occasion in 1971, was also a friend of Canada, but Mac's more positive reaction derived from his deeply held conviction that the ultimate worthiness of the purpose to be served may sometimes prevail over the customary requirements of form and precedent.

On this celebratory occasion, we rejoice that we were privileged to have known Mac so well, and to have been elevated by his legendary example of heart and mind. The great man has passed on, but his legacy is secure.

EMILE, B. KARSON, '51 LL.M., '53 J.S.D.
Studio City, California

Not only was he a great scholar and teacher, Mac was also a good man who helped a great number of American and foreign students in finding their professional destiny. I am certainly indebted to him for his advice and assistance for many years.

DINESH KHOSLA, '77 LL.M., '81 J.S.D.
Professor, CUNY, School of Law, Flushing, New York

Yale graduate students from all over the world called Professor Myres McDougal their teacher. So did I, despite the fact that he had "retired" from the Law School faculty a few months before my arrival from India. During our first encounter, when I addressed him as "Professor McDougal, Sir...," he gently put his hand on my arm and I heard a deep voice telling me, "let go of those British trappings young man, call me 'Mac.'" This simple statement broke all barriers of hierarchy and demolished all pretensions of power. When he learned that I had chosen to do my doctoral work in the area of human rights, he referred to a footnote in one of his books and commanded me to dig deeper into the traditions of human rights in the ancient Indian culture and teach it to others. He seemed particularly excited that I had chosen to conduct my research in the tradition of a legal sociologist. I was a bit surprised at his reaction since I was not using the Law, Science and Policy Model as I understood it then. But what mattered to him as a giant among great teachers was not the form but the substance and spirit of my work. He took immense pride and expressed his joy in the path I was charting for my life. The beauty of his relationship with me was that he never stopped coaxing me to continue to walk that path. A few years ago when my wife Savita and I established an annual human dignity award in memory of my father and to honor Professor McDougal for his lifelong commitment to the enhancement of human dignity, his simple words encouraging us to do more and follow our hearts captured the essence of a great teacher. Those words flashed in my mind when I learned that Mac had departed from our world. It has taken me over twenty-two years to address my teacher, my friend, as Mac.

JÜRGEN KÜHN, '55 LL.M.
Director-General, Federal Ministry of Economics, Bonn, Germany

I felt a great sadness when I was informed of the death of Professor McDougal. He has been one of the university teachers who influenced my life and my professional career most profoundly.

Myres Smith McDougal

ROBERT LAYTON, '54 LL.B.
Layton, Brooks & Hecht, New York, New York

I will always be indebted to him for many things other than the law teaching job he found for me two days after I got out of the Army in 1957.

EMANUEL MARGOLIS, '56

That was a great "debate" we had in the *Yale Law Journal* (1954), and some still believe I had the better of the argument! I miss you.

DAVID A. MARTIN, '75
Professor, University of Virginia School of Law, Charlottesville, Virginia

Like many that first day in Mac's international law class, I felt overwhelmed and intimidated by his energy, his self-assurance, and his powerful devotion to his subject and his causes. But before long we students caught some glimmer of what set Mac apart from most geopolitcians and, indeed, most international law scholars in those Cold War years. The next spring I tried—a novice's attempt—to capture that inchoate appreciation in the editors' introduction to a special *Law Journal* issue, honoring Mac on the occasion of his retirement from teaching (84 *Yale L.J.*, preceding page 961 (1975)):

> It is the "naked power boys," as Professor Myres McDougal calls them, who often insist that there is no such thing as international "law." Mac's lifetime efforts as a scholar and teacher refute that cynical assertion. He set out to show the essential characteristics of that aggregate of process we call law, and he has demonstrated how international law fits within that understanding.
>
> But this definitional victory is the smallest part of Mac's achievement. His conceptual framework reveals sharply law's potential as an alternative to naked power for the ordering of the world community. And, perhaps most importantly, his work stressed the responsibility of all—lawyers, government officials, scholars, citizens—to make the alternative yet more effective, but at the same time more completely committed to human dignity. In a world where the naked power boys occupy far too many seats of power, Mac's is a most refreshing, and sorely needed, ethical stance.

Mac's example and teaching served me well when I had the good fortune (nourished by Mac's support) to land a post in the State Department's brand-new Human Rights Bureau, and later to teach international law. Those experiences provided many opportunities to test what he taught, but my admiration for his insights and his passions has only grown. How rich we all are for having learned from him.

YOSHIHARU MATSUURA, '75 LL.M.
Professor of Law, Osaka University, Osaka, Japan.

He was an excellent teacher and first-rate scholar with formidable knowledge and wit. In 1975 I visited his office to say goodbye, for I completed my LL.M. course work and was ready to go home. He told me that I had been recommended to the J.S.D. program. Within a few minutes thought I decided to turn down this invitation. Since then, I had no chance to see him but I always remembered him and read his works. Though I did not become his disciple of the Law, Science and Policy School, I learned greatly and benefitted myself enormously from him.

JEREMIAH McKENNA, ESQ.

To Mac, You fought the good fight, you ran a good race, your heavenly crown was earned.

EDWARD W. McWHINNEY, QC, MP, '51 LL.M., '53 J.S.D.
House of Commons, Vancouver, British Columbia, Canada

He was a great scholar and an inspiring teacher, and also a warm, life-long friend for all his former students.

He had an unusual gift for identifying talent early and helping bright young people achieve their full potential.

VICENTE V. MENDOZA, '71 LL.M.
Associate Justice, Supreme Court of The Philippines, Manila, The Philippines

The academic world has lost a great teacher who has influenced generations of students not only in America but around the world.

Law, Science, and Policy, as McDougal called his jurisprudence, may have receded into history like other great movements in American law, but it succeeded in focusing attention on the need for training lawyers in policymaking. Myres McDougal and Harold Lasswell were the first to call for professional training in public policy, if the aim of legal education was not to be limited to production of legal technicians.

Beyond his inspired teaching which he elevated into a religion for democracy, McDougal will be remembered by his former students from abroad for his able chairmanship of the Yale Law School Committee on Graduate Studies. He did not only look after the welfare of foreign students, he followed their careers after they had returned to their countries. One day there was a notice for me on the bulletin board to see Professor McDougal immediately. It turned out he had read the appointment of Dean Vicente Abad Santos as Secretary of Justice in the Philippine Government. McDougal wanted to get confirmation of the news. For McDougal rejoiced at the successes of his former students.

I was glad I was able to pay Mac a visit at the Evergreen Woods Nursing Home in 1996. A resident said to me Mac was one person he was certain would be welcome in many countries in the world. I could not have agreed more. He gave the opinion on the basis of foreign visitors Mac had been receiving at the nursing home.

McDougal lives in the hearts and minds of countless students who consider him their teacher. No higher tribute can be paid to anyone than to be considered one's teacher.

ARTHUR M. MICHAELSON, '50 LL.B.
Hofheimer, Gartlir & Gross, New York, New York

He was a great man as well as a great teacher.

DODIE AND RICHARD S. MILLER, '59 LL.M.
Professor, University of Hawaii at Mānoa School of Law, Honolulu, Hawaii

Mac was a great and good friend to us. His teachings, when I was a graduate student in 1958–59, have been extraordinarily important to me, and have formed the basis for my view of law in the classroom and in my writings since then.

JOHN NORTON MOORE, '66
Professor, University of Virginia, School of Law, Charlottesville, Virginia

Mac is one of the most brilliant and creative legal scholars in the history of jurisprudence. Indeed, mere superlatives cannot begin to capture his achievements. Perhaps, however, my deliberate use of the present tense "is" in the first sentence in this paragraph conveys at least a small part of the reality. For

Mac's insights permeate all law today, and particularly his chosen field, international law. It has been said that each generation stands on the shoulders of the generation before. Mac's broad shoulders embrace much of modern international law and jurisprudence.

Mac the brilliant advocate, teacher and warm friend will be immensely missed. Mac's creativity and insights, however, are with us now and will be with each future generation. His contributions to the rule of law and human dignity will be part of the community of mankind always.

EDUARDO MORGAN, JR., '69 LL.M.
Morgan y Morgan, Panama City, Panama

It isn't easy to capture the memory in words of Mac. His dimension as a human being was so immense, covering so many things, that I don't know where to begin. The thing that struck you most about him after that first personal contact was his brilliance. McDougal was a genius and his mind was clear even in his ninety-first year when we paid him our last annual visit in October 1997.

That mind integrated a universe. McDougal did not tolerate barriers. His world had no boundaries—neither intellectual nor terrestrial. The superior intelligence and universal spirit, tied to a great kindness, made him a light and a magnet where hundreds of human beings from all parts of the world converged as his pupils. Mac's friendship was the common denominator for friendships among his many students and acquaintances.

McDougal became one of the most influential persons in the world. His network of international ex-alumni was comparable to a miniature version of the United Nations, where most of the countries were well represented by former students who became presidents, ambassadors, ministers, judges, practicing attorneys, and fellow scholars.

During my stay in Washington, I enjoyed, thanks to McDougal, a privilege shared by no other ambassador. President Clinton and his wife had been Mac's students and this simple fact made the ambassador of Panama someone special to them. In my last visit to Mac I was entrusted not only with delivering a personal greeting from the Clintons, but also with the assignment to bring back to them a report on the dear professor's health.

The greatest monument that the Yale Law School may erect for Mac will be the continuation of a post-graduate program of studies with broad participation of foreign students. Thus, our beloved school of law will continue being the center where ideas converge to help this globalized world be more just and democratic, the values that guided the life of Myres S. McDougal.

Myres Smith McDougal

EARL F. MURPHY, '55 LL.M., '59 J.S.D.
Professor, Ohio State University, Columbus, Ohio

When I received the J.S.D. degree in 1959, Mac said some most kind words about my work to my late mother. But he was so kind to all, that I could only hope what he then said was accurate. Certainly he was a most lovable man and—just about from the beginning of my acquaintance with him—he had my unremitting affection.

A man such as he deserved the greatest respect.

WINSTON P. NAGAN, '77 J.S.D.
Professor, University of Florida, College of Law, Gainesville, Florida

If Mac had any particularly distinctive characteristic in his relationship with other human beings, it was that he insistently tried to make the conception of human dignity and respect a significant part of those relationships. Because of that towering faculty, each of us has felt that our relationship with him is the most distinctive and indeed unique of his relationships. What is astounding is that these feelings could be so uniformly felt among all his friends, collaborators, and students. My relationship with Mac falls into the category of being both unique and distinctive, yet uniform in the larger circle of friends and collaborators.

When I came to the United States, I was privy to an animated discussion about a scholar named Harold Lasswell. The ideas discussed were not anything I had heard of previously. I should add that I knew nothing about such subversives as Freud, and had only the vaguest sense of the American revolution in the social sciences. I did have a sense of Oxbridge confidence that if I could find the Lasswell stuff, I could digest it effectively. Indeed, I thought that I might even actually find something that connected me more personally and deeply to the processes of forming a genuine intellectual identity. Thus, I began reading and not adequately understanding Lasswell's early writings on psychopathology and politics, world politics and personal insecurity, and a number of his now classical works.

When a young Yale doctoral student came to Duke on a research grant, he was surprised that I had been reading Lasswell and told me about the New Haven School. He, then, provided me with a complimentary copy of the famous Lasswell-McDougal-Reisman article in the Virginia journal dealing with the jurisprudence of international law. Since that experience I have never been able to look at anything in the conventional way that I had looked at things in the past.

When I came to Yale for a doctorate, Mac agreed to be my advisor, despite that fact that our first-ever interaction came when I challenged him in class. I did not realize at the time that this would be a life-defining event. From the moment I became Mac's student, I became aware of the scope and challenge of intellectual possibility. Like many, I was nurtured, cultivated, and given an intellectual spark—the kind of spark that I know burns within us all and which secures the presence of his spirit in all of us. My time at Yale under Mac was filled with excitement. The period of my J.S.D. work at Yale was also probably the happiest time of my life. I still stand in awe of Mac's generosity, big and small acts of kindness, as well as the constant dynamic of progressive challenge to the boundaries on the edge of the "known." I owe my intellectual identity, indeed my intellectual life, to him.

Perhaps an important insight that I garnered from my association with Mac was we must be hesitant, if not skeptical, about all contending paradigms of thinking, and that in working through and being self-aware of understanding the paradigm of thinking itself, one provides the greatest possible service that the intellect can give to society. What I found striking, especially in Mac's work, was his willingness to grapple explicitly with a plurality of forms of thinking as the essential engine or precondition to scholastic inquiry and enlightenment. Real policy thinking requires in short, a kind of revolution in how indeed we think. I had not early on appreciated how critical this was to Mac's outlook until he directed me to a careful study of Dewey's *How We Think*.

It is perhaps in this sense that one appreciates the limitations in law of both natural law and analytical positivism, which are rooted in a framework of intellectual skills, largely Aristotelian, that serve as a deep-structured limitation to understanding the problems of human beings in society and what the prospects are for what they might become. I would suggest that what McDougal has given us, and why it is so narrowly understood, is a very different form of thinking and inquiry, in which the cognitive faculties are to be liberated for the purpose of enlightening our understanding of the universe of social interaction. It is a form of cognition that is intrinsically curious and intellectually responsible.

Configurative thinking is the heart of configurative jurisprudence. Perhaps we have not contemplated more effectively the full implications of maximizing to the fullest measure all components of man's cognitive faculties, and to consider as well in this context the consistent, normative dimension of responsibility for values in the entire earth-space community. In this sense, I believe that Professor Falk, as far back as 1975, hit the nail on the head when he suggested that the most forthright appraisal of McDougal's jurisprudence is that it generated dangerous knowledge, and that in generating this kind of knowledge, he had constructed in effect a new paradigm for international legal studies. I would go further and suggest that future generations will look back on studies in law, science, and policy and hold that it was a new paradigm of thinking of millennial importance.

This frame is not designed, and cannot be designed, to produce safe and secure answers to all of the complex problems of world order, peace, and dignity. It is a powerful guide to relevant inquiry and responsible intervention; it is not a formula for rational absolutism.

Mac never could comprehend the prejudiced mind or the discrimination-prone personality. In fact, I think I can say without qualification that Mac did not think and could not think in "ethnic" or parochial terms. He was, in the finest sense of South African progressivism, the ultimate non-racial person. In this regard, he reminds me of Nelson Mandela who too, deep down in his core abhors racism and is the epitome of a non-racial perspective about world order. Mac never stopped pushing me to translate my ideas and thoughts into concrete action. He was the stimulus to Professor Jape Taylor and me in our efforts to establish an interdisciplinary peace and human rights institute in East Africa. The influence of his ideas which I used with abandon as chair of Amnesty International, USA, resulted in breaking the log jam on ratification of the Human Rights Treaties.

Mac enjoyed intellectual life as an arena of conflict and disputation, as well as construction and creativity. To ensure that we used our faculties to the fullest, he always moved the goal post a little further.

VED P. NANDA, '65
Professor of Law, University of Denver, College of Law, Denver, Colorado

I came to Yale because I wanted to work with Professor McDougal. Professor Brunson McChesney at Northwestern, where I was studying for my LL.M., was wholeheartedly in favor of the decision to move to Yale. I found Mac to be beyond my expectations—warm, generous, and enthusiastically supportive of his students. He always had time for you, no matter what he was doing when you knocked at his office door, and he always made students feel not just welcome but very important. During my first year in New Haven, Mac asked me to help a couple of other students who were not proficient in English, because he did not want them to fall behind.

As I was seeking a teaching position after leaving Yale, Mac could not have been more encouraging and helpful. He called deans and wrote letters, and I was fortunate to have several offers. When I chose the University of Denver, his advice was to go for a year and if I didn't like it I could move the next year. And here I am in Denver thirty-three years later.

We at Denver started the *Denver Journal of International Law and Policy* as a tribute to Mac and his focus on law and policy. The first issue was dedicated to him in 1972, and he honored us with his presence on the occasion of its publication. In 1976 our law school launched its annual Myres S. McDougal Distinguished Lecture Series in International Law and Policy, which celebrates its twenty-second anniversary this year. As a teacher and a scholar, he was undisputedly a giant in his field; and as a student of international law myself, my interest and appreciation in the subject were greatly enhanced. But my feelings for him are more of a personal nature, for I remember him as a guide and a friend.

Every year I would hear from Mac and speak with him over the phone whenever I needed guidance or advice. In his own genteel way, he even helped me and my wife, Katherine, get together. As a teacher, whenever I am ruffled and need some time for myself, if a student needs me, I recall Mac and try to emulate him in being able to find the necessary time to help.

I will sorely miss him.

M. NEAL NEWHOUSE, '91 LL.M.
Boise, Idaho

I met Mac at the first faculty reception of the new LL.M. candidates, which I believe took place even before school started. I was drawn to him, I suppose because I was of an age where he looked like a professor of law. I could tell he had so much interest in the students, the law, and the school.

On numerous occasions throughout the year when I could think of an excuse I would visit his office. It was stacked to the ceiling with articles and notes, and I would find an empty chair and seek his advice and counsel, of which he gave freely. He reminisced about Justice Douglas when he taught at Yale, and of his experiences in the Franklin Delano Roosevelt administration. I recall he told me his first love was property law, which was the field in which I hoped to teach, and that he had written a textbook shortly before World War II that "didn't sell very well because it had some positions that were a little too controversial for the time." I searched the library for a copy; I still have a summary of his views on private property rights, which are still controversial but no doubt represent the trend of the law.

Mac almost got me a job teaching, which I discovered after several years of trying without success would have been a miracle given the culture of law school faculties in this country (but that is the subject of another letter another day). It was during my interviews that I learned of his outstanding national and international reputation. Older members of law faculties all over the country stood in awe of Professor McDougal.

More than anyone else in your astounding and wonderful faculty, Mac made me think how different my life would have been had I applied (and been accepted) to attend Yale Law School in 1959. It would have been a challenge to try to get "honors" from the Professor!

I know Mac had a full and rich life and that is all we mortals can hope for in this life. But all of us who were touched by him along the way appreciate having known him, and feel the loss of a good friend and counselor.

CHARLES H. NORCHI, '89 LL.M.

My Yale teaching began with Yale residential college seminars. I asked Mac if he would be so kind as to guest lecture a class. He would grumble that Yale had put him out to pasture far too early and would be delighted to meet my students. One seminar was in Jonathan Edwards College, in an upper story seminar room which demanded negotiating a spiraling medieval staircase. The students were young undergraduates who had read portions of Mac's writings devoted to human rights and laws of war. They knew they would encounter a giant of international law. But when Mac appeared, slowly emerging from the dark spiral staircase the waiting students were in awe. For before them *was* a giant of a man, and he was far older than most of their grandparents. They were intimidated. Mac would launch into an overview of the New Haven School of Jurisprudence, and then begin asking questions. The students would eagerly respond and an animated discussion spanning three generations ensued. Mac never lost the teaching gift.

KEITH D. NUNES, '83 LL.M.

Professor, University of Orlando School of Law, Orlando, Florida

MEMORY HOLD THE DOOR FOR A MENSCH:
THE BLESSING OF MR. McDOUGAL

A remarkable and inspiring human being. A giant among men and women, whose astonishing career has earned him many tributes from Yale's deans, from Dean Eugene Rostow to Dean Harry Wellington to Dean Tony Kronman's sensitive and fascinating portrait that captures the whole man at last. His loyalty to "God, Country, and Yale" included his students from every imaginable background. I count my blessing for being just one of these students who work in the trenches.

Mr. McDougal stood for human rights, and he did not scrimp on matters as significant as that at all. His delightful friendliness, humor and charm came together in his graciousness to all he met. Good manners and hospitality of the South were in his sinews. Involved as he was in world shaping events and incidents of the home, he retained his graciousness and humor to contrast with deeply felt emotions. He had a fine feeling for people and was interested in the intellectual side as well as the relationship side of the person. Once while at his assisted living accommodation in Branford he must have seen some despondency in my face, when I thought I had let him down, and he gently turned to me and said: "Don't let life get you down, the world changes pretty quickly."

On another occasion he came to lecture to my human rights seminar in Yale College. Never eclipsed in his lifetime, the undergrads seemed to have a distinct sense that their own careers would progress just because of his presence and touch on them. They formed an immediate rapport with his easy, gracious and personable style of communication. Quite unintimidating to them, they were easily led into deep discussion with him and gave him a resounding ovation.

In the classroom, as in the human rights law course we student lawyers organized at the Law School along with the Lowenstein International Human Rights Law Project, Mr. McDougal was an enthusiast. He would set up a straw dog in some attention grabbing situation with the object of relating what he was talking about to a problem of society or community. The peacetime taking of hostages was such a case. He caused discussion because he maintained that "you've got to involve people in dialogue—in an active process." He inflamed his students with a desire to go further in jurisprudence and international law.

He used life at Yale to be open and inclusive to all the Maker's children from the Mississippi delta to the South African veldt. He perceived that consent and fair play is under-inclusive as a basis of human interaction. He perceived that law is a partial determinant of the physical and social environment if conceived of as rules. He, rather, sought to base the law as a powerful process of decision-making to offer a finite range of opportunities for action. He did that by defining law in terms of the opportunities individuals can conceive of making for themselves. He constrained individual freedom by limiting the range of opportunities in a social environment according to human dignity alone. His human freedom is always broad enough to allow people to make genuine choices. He did not require people to be good and to keep all promises to do good, moving our community to totalitarianism. Instead, he persuaded by letting the law leave us to be more or less virtuous in human dignity. He showed us that the law anywhere can be interpreted and applied to further individual purposes. He did not let their color, gender, or creed sway him from his goal of autonomy for the individual, empowering people to make choices and receive promises when they communicate decisions to act or refrain from acting in some definite way in the present or in the future.

No one went as far as he did for his students. His loyalty was consistent and undying. He was very proud of his photograph with the president of the United States, taken at the Oxford-Rhodes reunion. He would never fail to deflect adverse news of how the president was doing with a "He is a man close to the people and will do the right thing."

His passing is a sad moment. A time of a difficult transition for each of one of us who, in our great Republic and different parts of the world, consider him our intellectual father. So many of us were so deeply influenced and affected by Mac's intellectual and human mentorship. We can thank Hashem for being blessed for so many years by this inspiring teacher, and should be thankful for having had this experience … which he shared so unstintingly irrespective of creed or race. I retain a great love for an extraordinary man who made me feel so welcome in a place foreign to me and who liberated my mind after it had seen injustice.

Remembrances

CECIL J. OLMSTEAD, '52

To the memory of Mac which will always be bright.

ANDREW N. ONEJEME, '61 LL.M, '63 J.S.D.
Onejeme & Associates, Lagos, Nigeria

Mac was a great mentor and friend to many world-wide and if the voice of the people is still the voice of God, he is assured of eternal rest in the bosom of the Lord Almighty.

Mac touched many lives in his native America and in virtually all parts of the world. His memory will remain evergreen and indeed unforgettable, which is the tonic that tempers in some measure the sadness we feel by his passing. May his affectionate and gentle soul rest in peace.

IVAN PADJEN
Editor, Croatian Critical Law Review, Zagreb, Croatia

I have always admired Professor McDougal's scholarship, but since 1990 I have been also fortunate enough to know him personally. He had become my great teacher and a very dear friend. I am sure that all of us who came in contact with Professor McDougal will long cherish his memory.

JORDAN J. PAUST, '74

I was fortunate to see Mac during the last few days of his long, productive and remarkable life. Mac spoke slowly in comparison to the vigor of the scholar-advocate that we remember in an LSP seminar (for me, during the early 70's) and during robust interchanges at American Society of International Law and International Law Association meetings. If he did not win each of those intellectual battles, he always made his points known. Now, he rested often. His voice reflected his calm, pensive nature and concern for yet another member of his "family" who had come to say goodbye. "Jordan, I don't know what to say." "There is no need to say anything, Mac," I tried to assure him, quietly holding his hand. He responded, clasping mine. We had been close for so long, but words never had been necessary to reassure our relationship. I remembered Mac in his office at Yale and the first time I saw him at his desk. One had to navigate past book shelves and a maze of papers stacked on tables to discover where the "Yes!" had come from. He couldn't see perfectly then, but Mac could pull a paper that I might "find useful" from the top third of one of those stacks, as if by magic! Fewer books were in the room where he lay, but they were there along with a yearbook from the University of Mississippi, letters from presidents, and the many expressions of concern from his extended family. He was comfortable and retained the great dignity of the gentleman scholar, the father, for some, or grandfather that we knew. He was still attentive to his former students, still wanting to communicate a very personal, reassuring message to those close to him. "The passing of an era," Siegfried noted sadly when we had walked outside the room. If not an era, the passing of a great human being. "God loves you Mac," I told him. Surely I was right.

ELLEN ASH PETERS, '54 LL.B.
Senior Justice, Connecticut Supreme Court
Professor (Adjunct) of Law, Yale Law School

Every day of my life as a law student, teacher and judge was enriched—as you promised it would be, by your teaching in Property I.

GEORGE P. PODOLIN
Co-Editor in Chief, Yale Journal of International Law

Our journal was founded to memorialize Professor McDougal's scholarship in the "New Haven School." We continually strive to live up to his legacy.

LOUIS H. POLLAK, '48 LL.B.
Former Dean, Yale Law School
Senior Judge, U. S. District Court for the Eastern District of Pennsylvania

Gratefully, with a world of thanks and praise for my teacher, colleague, and friend.

HORTON R. PRUDDEN, SR., '47
CEO First Southeast Corporation, Palm Beach, Florida

I loved Mr. Mac and he brought the legal world into air rights twenty-five years early.

Remembrances

K. VENKATA RAMAN, '67 J.S.D.
Professor, Queen's University, Kingston, Canada

Mac was a wonderful person, a truly great scholar, and I am sure he will come to be reckoned by successive generations even more as a great jurist of the twentieth century.

PEMMARAJU S. RAO, '68 LL.M., '70 J.S.D.
Legal Adviser, Ministry of Foreign Affairs, India
Member, International Law Commission, United Nations

I was deeply grieved to learn of the end of a great master of international law and of an even greater scholar and teacher and, above all, a human being *par excellence,* the likes of him we rarely encounter.

Like many, many of his students, I am privileged to be touched by his greatness. "Mac" was a legend in his own time and will be for a long, long time to come.

LEO J. RASKIND, '55 LL.B.
Emeritus Professor of Law, University of Minnesota

Mac's maxim: "Nothing is too much for a friend."

HERBERT K. REIS, '57
Adjunct Professor of Law, New York Law School, New York, New York

I came to know Mac best when he was teaching at New York Law School, for he would come down to New York City, where I was long posted as legal advisor to the U.S. Delegation to the U.N., and we would dine at the Yale Club or the Oyster Bar. Mac helped me greatly in, finally, reaching a decision to teach, though as an adjunct only, which I did for some eighteen years at NYU Law School. And Mac's stimulation!—I have the most lovely memories.

LISA REISMAN

Mac, I carry with me the sage advice you shared with me throughout my life.

DAVID A. RUTTENBERG, '61 LL.B.
Wolf, Haldenstein, Adler, Freeman & Hertz, New York, New York

My experience with Professor McDougal was, as I am certain it was for all of his students, a most rewarding and exciting educational and personal experience.

JOVITO R. SALONGA, '49 J.S.D.
Mandaluyong City, The Philippines

Professor McDougal was my professor in international law in 1948. His policy-oriented approach has shaped my outlook on law and other related disciplines, which is why his departure diminishes us all who came under his influence. Beyond the Law School, he followed my academic and political career over the years with great interest.

OTTO SANDROCK, '56 LL.M.
Professor, Universität Münster, Münster, Germany

Mac was a great teacher and scholar, and I appreciate the deep personal relations which he always maintained with his disciples all over the world.

HARRY CARL SCHAUB, '55

Indirectly, it was because of Myres McDougal that I decided to apply to Yale Law School in 1949. At the College of the University of Pennsylvania, Professor Robert Shelton (later to teach at the University of Wisconsin Law School) regularly extolled during his pre-law course the innovative scholarship of our faculty, especially Mr. McDougal's. By the time I arrived here, he seemed like the old friend that he later became.

The first classes of Property I were a rude awakening, as he proceeded to demolish the faulty positions and feeble arguments of the first-year students. His method could conceal his warmth and charm for only a short period, but his questioning approach to black-letter law remains with us all.

In time, as we got to know each other in a number of his international law and policy courses, I knew that he was genuinely interested in my development as a scholar, as a lawyer, and as a person.

Earlier this year I was deeply moved when I received from his assistant my original paper submitted in his seminar in the Spring of 1995. His scholarship, probing mind, generosity and warmth remain with me.

LUIS SCHUCHINSKI, '64
Vice President, Taxes, Bestfoods, Englewood Cliffs, New Jersey

He was indeed a great international law scholar, legal philosopher, and human being.

I was a beneficiary, perhaps, a prime example, of Mac's personal help. As a young lawyer in the post-Castro Havana of 1960 I was determined to leave the country and became a lawyer in the U.S. Mac played a pivotal role in my career. His counsel and intervention proved invaluable. I was later fortunate to work with him on research projects and this became a wonderful legal education all by itself.

Thus, the single feature of this great man that I will remember most vividly is his unconditional generosity. Once he offered his support it became unwavering. Indeed, I know that he was particularly helpful to his former students during their difficult times. He also keenly and quietly enjoyed their successes.

I will forever remember him with affection.

STEPHEN M. SCHWEBEL, '54 LL.B.
President, International Court of Justice, The Hague, The Netherlands

He was a man whose heart was as great as his mind. I shall always think of him with the deepest affection as well as admiration.

ARDEN E. SHENKER, '62 LL.B.
Tooze, Shenker, Duden, et al., Portland, Oregon

Some of my fondest post-law school memories have to do with continuing contact I was able to enjoy with Myres McDougal. We all miss him.

HUBERT F. SONTHEIM, '52 LL.M.
Director, FSC Summit Trust S.A., Nyon, Switzerland

My year at the Law School was intellectually a most stimulating year to which Mac contributed in a major way. With a great deal of understanding and tolerance he knew how to challenge his students. Our relationship developed into a deep friendship which has never receded. I will miss Mac. My affectionate thoughts always will be for him.

CHARLES W. T. STEPHENSON, '59 LL.B.
Office of the General Counsel, Agency for International Development,
Washington, D.C. (Retired)

Karl Linnaeus, a great figure in the history of science, invented the system of binomial classification, in which all plants and animals are given two Latin names, for genus and species, to identify their relationships and differences. We are *homo sapiens.* Myres McDougal and Harold Lasswell have done the same thing, in English, in a carefully chosen vocabulary that can be applied to illuminate, and compare, the context of any areas where making policy choices is needed. The two of them left everything they touched a little more sapient.

H. PETER STERN, '54 LL.B.

Mac was an intellectual inspiration and close friend, always stimulating and original, and on the mark.

ROBERT B. STEVENS, '58 LL.M.
Master, Pembroke College, Oxford University, Oxford, United Kingdom

In many ways I felt culturally close to Myres McDougal. It was not so much that we had both been at Oxford and that we overlapped with some of the same teachers and certainly had much the same educational experience, but I felt an affinity for his background as a son of a rural doctor in Mississippi. I know that sounds odd, but as I learned when I was at Tulane, there is a surprising similarity between rural Mississippi and middle England. And in that sense I think I understood him.

I certainly could not say that when I arrived at Yale. I had had the worst possible English legal education. Oxford at that time was in its period of high formalism. The teaching of law was almost by rote. It would be difficult to imagine a less intellectual subject. Of course I did not really realise how bad the education had been and I did not warm to Myres' high scepticism. It seemed so inelegant compared with high formalism. I did not always respond well to his criticisms of me or the system.

Over my year as a graduate student, however, he came to have a profound effect on my thinking. I disagreed with so much of his approach—I never got to love the social science jargon—but as I look back on it, I realise that that year was immensely significant for me; indeed, probably the most significant force in my education.

Of course I was then a colleague for nearly twenty years. Again we clashed on various things—frequently on personnel issues—but on so much I learned to admire and respect him. Needless to say, like all of his students, I maintained a level of affection which has never left me.

GERALD A. SUMIDA, '69
Carlsmith, Ball, Wichman, Case & Ichiki, Honolulu, Hawaii

A giant has passed from amongst all of us. He was in many respects larger than life, but for me always remained the preeminent scholar, teacher, and friend who, when I went to Yale at the urging of Dick Falk, took me under wing as soon as I renewed my acquaintanceship with him during my earliest days at Yale Law School.

RICHARD A. THIGPEN, '69 LL.M.
Professor, University of Alabama, Tuscaloosa, Alabama

He was among the great figures of the last half century, and before, in his contributions to public policy and law, higher education, and conceptual understanding affecting the world arena; and his good influence will be deeply missed. His work will live on by and through former students, associates, and colleagues over the world.

FREDERICK S. TIPSON, '71 M.A.
International Relations, Hongkong Telecom, Quarry Bay, Hong Kong, China

I find it hard to speak of Mac with calmness or detachment;
This man—this place—evoke for me a special old attachment.
Within these halls I first explored that promising alliance,
Between the ends of policy and those of social science.
Like those who came before and since, I rallied to the bugle,
Which summoned young and restless souls to Lasswell and McDougal.

I came in '69 in International Relations:
An innocent in grad school with expectant expectations.
I never had intended to be drawn into "the Law":
The catalog was then the dullest thing I ever saw.
I couldn't quite imagine how a healthy young adult,
Could spend three precious years of life on subjects so occult;

Myres Smith McDougal

Boys and girls who should be doing poetry or sports,
Were sitting still to garner in property and torts.

But then I chanced to notice as I waded through the list,
A Law School course which seemed to have an innovative twist,
(And, no doubt, seemed to promise comprehensiveness and unity),
Its title was "The Public Order of the World Community."

Myres McDougal taught the course, though half-way through he left;
His eye required surgery—but lest we feel bereft,
Michael Reisman filled the void and hardly missed a beat;
If anything, he made that course a double-barreled treat.

I must have done my homework and I must have talked in class well,
Because before I knew it, I was writing stuff for Lasswell:
A major theoretician, who was then still in his prime,
Expounding on the global "Revolution of our Time."
I took three other courses and became a strong supporter,
Of politics and law recast toward global public order.
In contrast to the scientism then around "I.R."
"Law, Science and Policy" was major C.P.R.
Teaching lawyers not to be just clever, but constructive;
And showing how decisions should be socially productive.

For Mac it was a mission, which he undertook with glee,
(If Lasswell was the princess, then McDougal was the pea),
Relishing the chance to take some prof or judge to task,
(While Harold made ingredients, Mac mixed them in the flask),
Transforming legal doctrine from analyses of rules,
And rescuing international law from cranks, and knaves and fools.

Perhaps I was too vulnerable, or simply mesmerized,
But I was also changed by them, expanded and revised.
Mac and Harold—yes, and Michael—painted me a picture,
Which ever after in my life has been a constant fixture:
An enterprise of systematic insights and creations:
The shaping of a framework for the shaping of relations.
A way of looking at the world, a basic orientation,
That framed for me a kind of lifelong course of contemplation.

Later, at Virginia, and with John Moore as a coach,
I wrote a dissertation on the whole "Yale School" approach.

Remembrances

Arguing that, rather than a radical creation,
Their enterprise was based upon a long and rich foundation:
From Dewey's pragmatism to Chicago's social science,
Beyond the Legal Realists and their critical defiance.
Thus viewed in larger context, many minds of notoriety,
Had underpinned their "Jurisprudence for a Free Society."

Essential to their work is that it wasn't just reflective,
They saw its realization in the goals of the collective;
A common dedication to a set of valued ends;
A team of social engineers, a meeting ground of friends.

I spent countless hours reading Reisman, Moore, and Falk,
I wonder why my wife did not just up and "take a walk"?
Many months she shared her life with Harold, Mac and *moi;*
I know she must have wearied of this dull *menage a trois.*
We even had a billy goat I gave the name of Mac.
(I tried to call him Lasswell, but he wouldn't answer back.)

So when that work was finished, and I wrote the dedication,
Of course, it went "To Laura:" who sustained my aspiration,
"For evenings dull and weekends frugal,
With me and Lasswell and McDougal."

I soon joined a Senate staff and then the private sector,
Equipped with mental models as a constant course corrector;
Alert for faulty frameworks and for incomplete assumptions,
Seeking out revisions and reversals of presumptions.

And yet, with Mac, I'd take the tack that what I think of now,
Is not just *what* he taught me then—no, not just what, but *how.*
The mentor as fomenter, as inducer of invention,
Accelerator, challenger, rejecter of convention.
Loyal to his students, with an interest quite paternal,
Conveying to them all a sense that learning is fraternal.

And so now—thirty years beyond—I find that, looking back,
The mentor *is* the message—that I also learned from Mac.

ROBERT C. TRAVIS, '62 LL.M.
Jackson, Mississippi

I received notice of Professor Myres McDougal's death with an extremely heavy heart. He was the reason I ever attended Yale Law School, and he was just about the finest man I was ever privileged to know. Myres was a native Mississippian and a friend of my late father, Cecil F. Travis (Class of 1926), so our relationship went back a long way. I shall miss him.

His death and his passing certainly mark the end of an era for the Law School. He brought world-wide prestige and status to the Law School. As you well know no man ever did more in so many areas of the law, while at the same time always finding time to help "one of his own." He was quite a man indeed.

JAN F. TRISKA, '50 LL.M., '52 J.S.D.
Professor, Stanford University,
Department of Political Science, Stanford, California (Retired)

He was a demanding but kind teacher and a great human being. He has been influential on my way of thinking these many years.

ROBERT F. TURNER
Professor, University of Virginia, School of Law, Charlottesville, Virginia

The world has lost its finest international lawyer. We have lost a great human being and friend.

IVAN A. VLASIC, '58 LL.M., '61 J.S.D.
Professor Emeritus of Law, McGill University, Montreal, Quebec, Canada

I first came in contact with Mac in his Law, Science and Policy course (September 1957), which he shared with (perennially absent) Harold Lasswell. From my application form seeking admission to the Graduate Program, he learned that I had an LL.M. degree in air law, in addition to a couple of publications on air transport law. Rather early in the term, he called on me in the classroom of some sixty students to answer a question, but first introducing me as an "expert in air law". To the best of my ability I attempted to answer the question but was quickly interrupted by Mac's "No, no, you are all wrong." Needless to say, I was deeply embarrassed. The same thing happened the very next class, when again my unfinished answer was summarily dismissed. From that day until the end of the course, whenever asked for an opinion, I would shout "I don't know." This side of public McDougal was well known to all those who attended the annual meetings of the American Society of International Law. Mac's participation in the ASIL proceedings was for years the highlight of the event. Whether he was a panelist or merely a "voice from the floor," his presence guaranteed that there would be only standing room for all those who wanted to witness Mac's cutting wit and uniquely original approach to international law. He was feared and admired in his inimitable (some might say—intolerant) way of dealing with opinions on some issue or concept of international law at variance with his own interpretation. These two illustrations show the public side of Mac, as I saw it.

His other side was very different—he was warm, unselfish, generous, and immensely helpful to his students and collaborators, with many of whom he kept in touch until his death. In his comportment (and language) Mac was to me a true Southern gentleman, in the best sense of that expression.

During my three years of close, indeed, daily contacts with Mac I profited greatly from his encyclopedic knowledge of the law, his ideas about the function of law in international society, and his incredible working discipline. Never have I met a scholar with such zest for work as Mac; his idea of a great day was when he could work undisturbed for sixteen or more hours.

When the work on our *Law and Public Order in Space* commenced (1959–60), Mac was already working with his collaborators (Feliciano and Burke) on two seminal books (*Law and Minimum World Public Order,* 1961 and *The Public Order of the Oceans,* 1962). As was his custom, we started with the preparation of an exhaustive outline, which eventually consisted of forty-five pages. The objective of our joint effort, as decreed at the outset by Mac, was to write the best and most comprehensive treatise on the emerging law of outer space. At least in the assessment of Sir Wilfred Jenks, himself a superior legal scholar, our volume represented a landmark which will be difficult to better. The book was eventually reviewed in at least forty periodicals. Although a highly specialized volume, dealing with a novel branch of law, it went into two printings, totaling some 4,000 copies, long sold out.

I believe that *Law and Public Order in Space,* being the first comprehensive publication in the field, had a considerable impact on subsequent scholarship and at least some influence on the practice of states.

Let me say, in conclusion, that words cannot fully express the debt I owe to Myres McDougal who was a devoted friend and by far the most important teacher in my academic career.

GEORGE K. WALKER, '76
Professor, Wake-Forest University, School of Law, Winston-Salem, North Carolina

Mac had retired by the time I spent that good year at Yale, but he was always encouraging during those guerilla warfare years in legal education, ready with good advice; he was an excellent mentor. We chuckled about having grown up fifty or so miles apart—Mac in Tupelo, Mississippi, and me as a biology professor's son in Tuscaloosa, Alabama—but the difference in our ages we never noticed or let get between us. Beginning at Virginia, continuing at Yale and on to this day, I remain grateful for the exposure to his ideas and methodology, which help in research, thinking and writing.

RUTH WEDGWOOD, '76
Professor of Law, Yale Law School

The New Haven School encompassed more than international law—but the core of realism itself.

DAVID WEILD, '59 LL.B.

To "Mac": In many ways the greatest "bread and butter" lawyer of them all; mentor and friend. Many thanks.

BURTON M. WEINSTEIN, '56

The magnitude of Mississippi's gift to Yale (and the world) offsets a lot of others it has inflicted. With respect and affection for the skill and enlightenment.

WALTER O. WEYRAUCH, '62 J.S.D.
Professor, University of Florida, College of Law, Gainesville, Florida

When I think of Mac, I think of him as a humanist, a man of great learning in the classical tradition, a teacher of Greek and Latin, and a graduate of Oxford. My imagery is closely tied to personal experiences that I had and also to his fundamentally academic and humanitarian orientation. The policy sciences approach is, from my perspective, a manifestation of these character traits.

Mac, as a legal scholar, was also primarily an academic. I mean this in the sense of a pursuit of truth for its own sake. In the American culture, many colleagues in law teaching, though highly intelligent, are essentially displaced lawyers who find themselves in a university setting, but whose identifications are outside of the academy. To me, coming from Europe and being intrigued by what I perceived to be odd and repressive customs of learning, meeting Mac was like breathing fresh air. Here was a truly educated man, under any standard, who had the capacity to judge his students' worth by engaging them in conversation. He dismissed the incidents of formal merit as developed by educational bureaucracies. He had retained the ability to observe, to think and to evaluate. The dehumanizing aspects of American academic life were foreign to his pursuit of truth and basic humanism.

In short, I experienced Mac as a warm and friendly person who, while I talked with him, was wholly absorbed by what I said and did and who was interested in me as a fellow human being, as he was with anyone whom he had contact. For this my heartfelt thanks!

SIEGFRIED WIESSNER, '83 LL.M.
Professor, St. Thomas University, School of Law, Miami, Florida

PROFESSOR MYRES SMITH McDOUGAL: A TENDER FAREWELL

When my good friend Keith Nunes first introduced me to the "New Haven Approach," I found it a revelation, an intellectual rebirth. As a European student of law, in particular international law, I found the discipline oftentimes barren, mechanically conceptual. Traditional positivists, for example, counted up countries' support for an alleged "rule" of customary law in order to document what they considered necessary "state practice." To me, this approach to law resembled the attitude of stamp collectors toward their treasures rather than an enlightened scholar's proper understanding of his or her intellectual tasks. It appeared narrow-minded and retrospective, geared toward the digesting and manipulating of paper renditions of decisions of the past. Coming to Yale, studying with Michael Reisman, participating in his class on Public Order in the World Community, and dissecting theory in his seminar on Jurisprudence, was, thus, an intellectual liberation.

One day, Michael introduced me to the person who had developed the new role of the professional in the law that I always had, unconsciously, aspired to emulate: Myres Smith McDougal. His office was located directly below my student room at the Yale Law School. Professor McDougal, in these early '80s, still cut an awe-inspiring presence both professional and personal. Though he retired from teaching at the Yale Law School in the spring of 1974, he continued to teach at New York Law School for at least ten more years, and blessed many more students there with the gifts of his mind and his heart. Those gifts were abundant, and he shared them abundantly. The wisdom of his many years of study and research, his eagerness of, and fondness for, intellectual exchange, his humility and openness for persons from all walks of life, his kind words for, and genuine interest in, the students who came from every corner of the globe, made him a friend for, and beyond, life.

Intellectually, Myres McDougal was a true "founder" of jurisprudence. Together with his lifelong collaborator, Harold D. Lasswell, he transcended sterile positivism with a few, but potent, basic ideas, and their complex, but appropriately comprehensive, implementation: (1) that law is an ongoing process of authoritative and controlling decision; (2) that it is not limited to commands of the sovereign crystallized in "rules;" (3) that it addresses societal problems, constituted by conflicting claims; (4) that these claims, and past and future authoritative and controlling responses to them, have to be analyzed rigorously and contextually, using all disciplines of knowledge at our disposal; and (5) that, from this analysis, an answer to the societal problem under investigation should be developed and advocated using, as a guiding light, the goals of a public order of human dignity. In short, Myres Smith McDougal stood for, and developed, a much-needed problem- and policy-oriented approach to law. Along the way, he developed a theory of interdisciplinary research and linked it to a most fruitful redefinition of the idea of a lawyer. He embodied the ideal of the lawyer-statesman. Had he the power, he would have been the model philosopher-king. As a committed democrat, however, he saw his role in trying to reason with people, trying to convince them that the solution he recommended was the best in the context addressed. It was the one that maximized all peoples' (minorities included!) access to all that humans value. In these days of blatant fights for selfish interest, his eye and his aspiration for the common good will be missed dearly.

Those who take up his challenge, though, are not lawyers lost. The idea of the nobile officium of lawyers, and, in particular, law professors, was one Myres McDougal lived with unfailing elegance and Southern poise. If anybody could embody the quest for a public order of "human dignity," McDougal did. I owe him a debt of gratitude for his advice so warmly given, his words of support in times of doubt, his "unconditional love." Through his paper on nationality and human rights, he helped me conceive my doctoral thesis. His constant advice and encouragement brightened the day and allowed for the blossoming of ideas otherwise foreclosed. In many ways, even though my thesis was completed at a German university, Professor McDougal was my real *Doktorvater*.

Later, he asked me to work with him on various projects, an honor I will treasure forever. In the summer of 1991, a very hot and humid one, he had taken seriously ill. He had just been chosen to be the first recipient of the Cordell Hull Award at Cumberland Law School in Birmingham, Alabama. He was confined to his bed at his home in New Haven's St. Ronan Street and could not make the trip to the ceremony. He asked me to present the Cordell Hull Lecture and accept the award in his place. I will never forget the Southern hospitality and warm reception I received from Dean Parham Williams and his distinguished institution that day. Professor McDougal was truly loved. Needless to say, Parham also was one of his devoted students and friends.

On a broader scope, I had the pleasure of working with Professor McDougal on the introduction to the reissue of his 1961 magnum opus, with Florentino Feliciano, on *Law and Minimum World Public Order*. The Cold War had just come to a close, and we had a chance to assess the contours of the incipient "new world order." We did have our share of disagreements, some over policy in individual contexts, some over style. Nonetheless, Professor McDougal always listened and levelled with me, never forcing his opinion ex cathedra. He wished to convince, not coerce. Similarly, minimum public order, in his view, was not sustainable without the aspiration for optimum order: peace, ultimately, was one side of the coin, and respect for human rights and dignity the necessary other.

It was gratifying to see Professor McDougal recover from the terrible summer of 1991. Yale New Haven Hospital and the Evergreen Nursing Home gave him the support he needed to continue his work, to complete its summa, *Jurisprudence for a Free Society,* and, most of all, to bless us with his smile, his gentleness, his affection. The travels from Miami to Evergreen, however, became ever more urgent.

Last May, ... as the candle of life of this great man flickers and fades, we touch his hand and know we'll never be apart. Myres McDougal is a part of us, and we, certainly, are a part of him.

Myres Smith McDougal

SOPHIA TIERONG ZHU
(Spouse of Ifan Chang, '48 J.S.D.), Hunan, Peoples' Republic of China

During our two years in New Haven (1946–1948), my husband Ifan Chang and I had many friends. Professor McDougal of Yale Law School was the most unforgettable person to us. We were introduced to him by our good friend Jimmy Johnson of Cleary, Gottlieb, Steen & Hamilton, Mac's good friend and student. So we had the pleasure to visit him and his family when we arrived in New Haven and were often invited for meals with him, Frances, and Johnny.

Ifan got his LL.B. in Suzhou Law School in Shanghai and practiced law for several years there. He was admitted into Yale Law School in 1947. At that time there was a group of foreign students pursuing graduate studies under the supervision of Mac, approximately twenty graduate students from England, France, Czechoslovakia, Palestine, India, China, etc. Mac was Ifan's advisor. Ifan often told me that Mac was an authority on international law, a good legal educator, an excellent teacher and a sincere friend to his students. All the graduate students respected and loved him very much. His world community approach—the sharing of values—made a deep impression on my mind. He was very knowledgeable, but he was very approachable. Ifan was very grateful to Mac for his instruction, help, and support. I was very thankful to him for his friendship.

After our return to China we corresponded with Mac. Then there came a period when we could not communicate with him. In 1957 Ifan voiced his opinion in the provincial PPCC that there should be rule of law instead of rule of man. He was severely criticized by an article in the City's Party evening paper. At that time he had diabetes and was hospitalized. Knowing that he was misunderstood and that in his health he could not stand criticism and denunciation at meetings, he jumped into the Xiang River. It was certainly very difficult for me to stand such suffering. I myself was in great trouble and was labeled as an ultrarightist (Both my problems and his were clarified in 1979 and 1983. We were redressed and our reputations rehabilitated.)

After the reestablishment of Sino-American diplomatic relations, I wrote the first letter to Mac, and he replied to me on June 13, 1979: "Your letter is a voice from a very distant but happy past. I have often thought of Ifan and you and wondered how you were faring. There are many rumors, all apparently untrue. I am sorry to hear of Ifan's passing, you will remember that I had great affection for him. I congratulated you upon your son and hope that your grandchild has safely arrived." It was very moving to have received word from him. Later on in 1988 I sent him my autobiography and asked him to send a copy of Ifan's biography to the Yale Law School. He replied on October 12,

1988: "I have read your story with tremendous interest both because it is about you and because of the very different culture of which you write. You write, as you think, beautifully and perceptively. I marvel that, after so many hard times and difficulties, you still have such great spirit. It is remarkable that you have survived, nevertheless remained optimistic. The Yale University Library has asked for all my papers. Your statement will be among these papers. What you write should be of interest to historians of China."

I have also found that he wrote me on March 28, 1988 regarding Ifan's biography: "It is a most fascinating and moving history. It makes the events live even for one who has no previous acquaintance with many of the names and places. It is obvious that you and Ifan had a both difficult and exciting time in those years of turmoil, and that many people suffered many hardships. I was much moved by the details about Ifan and you have deep sympathy still for all that transpired." His words gave me great encouragement and moral support. We corresponded with each other continuously and exchanged Xmas greetings almost every year except when he was quite ill.

We have a saying in China that there is no feast in the world that has no ending. It is true. But Mac will live in my heart forever and I will always remember his help and encouragement to me, his contribution to legal education, and the influence of his world community approach to peace.

VITA & BIBLIOGRAPHY

Born November 23, 1906, Burton, Mississippi; B.A., M.A., University of Mississippi, 1927; LL.B., University of Mississippi, 1935; B.A. in Jurisprudence, B.C.L., Oxford University, England, 1930; J.S.D., Yale Law School, 1931; Assistant Professor of Law, University of Illinois, 1931–1934; Associate Professor, Yale Law School, 1934–1939; Professor, Yale Law School, 1939–1975; William K. Townsend Professor of Law, 1944–1958; Sterling Professor of Law, 1958–1975; Distinguished Visiting Professor of Law, New York Law School, 1976–1985; Attorney, Assistant General Counsel Lend-Lease Administration, 1942; General Counsel, Office of Foreign Relief and Rehabilitation Operations, State Department, 1943; Lecturer, Fulbright Conference on American Studies, Cambridge University, 1952; Visiting Professor of Law, Cairo University, 1959–1960; Occasional Lectures: The Hague Academy of International Law, the United States Naval War College, the National War College, the Army War College, the Air University; Member of Board of Editors: The American Journal of International Law; The American Journal of Jurisprudence; Member: American Bar Association; American Society of International Law (President 1958, Honorary President 1973–1976); Association of American Law Schools (President 1966); American Academy of Arts and Sciences; U.S. Delegation, United Nations Conference on the Law of Treaties, Vienna, 1969; U.S. Panel, The Permanent Court of Arbitration, 1963–1969; Member of the Institut de Droit International; Kappa Sigma, Mason; Clubs: Graduate, Lawn (New Haven); Yale (New York City); Cosmos (Washington, D.C.).

Honors and Awards: Doctor of Humane Letters, Columbia, 1954; LL.D., Northwestern University, 1966; LL.D., York University (Canada), 1970; LL.D., University of New Haven, 1975; L.H.D., Temple University, 1975; Hudson Medal, American Society of International Law, 1976; Honorary Fellow, St. John's College, University of Oxford, 1982; Read Medal, Canadian Council on International Law, 1985; Hull Medal, Samford University, Cumberland School of Law, 1991. Medal of Merit, Yale Law School Alumni Association, 1992, Honorary Doctorate, University of the Philippines, 1994; Lifetime Achievement Award, University of Mississippi, 1996.

Myres Smith McDougal
BOOKS

Municipal Land Policy and Control (New York: Practising Law Institute, 1946).

The Case for Regional Planning, with Special Reference to New England, (Report of Directive Committee on Regional Planning) (1947) (with Maurice Rotival).

Property, Wealth, Land: Allocation, Planning and Development; Selected Cases and Other Materials on the Law of Real Propety (Charlottesville, VA: Michie Casebook Corp., 1948) (with David Haber).

McDougal & Associates, *Studies in World Public Order* (New Haven, CT: Yale University Press, 1960), reprinted with new introduction (New Haven, CT: New Haven Press and Dordrecht, The Netherlands: Martinus Nijhoff Publishers, 1986).

Law and Minimum World Public Order: The Legal Regulation of International Coercion (New Haven, CT: Yale University Press, 1961) (with Florentino P. Feliciano), reprinted with new introduction and new title, *The International Law of War: Trasnational Coercion and World Public Order* (New Haven, CT: New Haven Press and Dordrecht, The Netherlands: Martinus Nijhoff Publishers, 1994).

The Public Order of the Oceans: A Contemporary International Law of the Sea (New Haven, CT: Yale University Press, 1962) (with William T. Burke), reprinted with new introduction (New Haven, CT: New Haven Press and Martinus Nijhoff Publishers, 1987).

Law and Public Order in Space (New Haven, CT: Yale University Press, 1963) (with Harold D. Lasswell & Ivan A. Vlasic).

The Interpretation of Agreements and World Public Order: Principles of Content and Procedure (New Haven, CT: Yale University Press, 1967) (with Harold D. Lasswell & James C. Miller), reprinted with new introduction and new title, *The Interpretation of International Agreements and World Public Order: Principles of Content and Procedure* (New Haven, CT: New Haven Press and Dordrecht, The Netherlands: Martinus Nijhoff Publishers, 1994).

Human Rights and World Public Order: The Basic Policies of an International Law of Human Dignity (Yale University Press, 1980) (with Harold D. Lasswell & Lung-chu Chen).

International Law in Contemporary Perspective (Mineola, NY: The Foundation Press, Inc., 1981) (with W. Michael Reisman).

International Law Essays: A Supplement to International Law in Contemporary Perspective (Mineola, NY: The Foundation Press, Inc., 1981) (with W. Michael Reisman).

Power and Policy in Quest of Law: Essays in Honor of Eugene Victor Rostow (Dordrecht, The Netherlands: Martinus Nijhoff Publishers, 1985) (co-edited with W. Michael Reisman).

Jurisprudence For a Free Society: Studies in Law, Science & Policy (New Haven, CT: New Haven Press and Dordrecht, The Netherlands: Martinus Nijhoff Publishers, 1992) (with Harold D. Lasswell).

Jurisprudence For a Free Society: Studies in Law, Science & Policy (Dordrecht, The Netherlands: Martinus Nijhoff, 1992) (with Harold D. Lasswell) (Special, unabridged, student edition, 1997).

ARTICLES

"Bankruptcy," 3 *Encyclopedia Britannica* 100 (14th rev. ed. 1936) (with William O. Douglas).

"Land Title Transfer: A Regression," 48 *Yale Law Journal* 1125 (1939) (with John W. Brabner-Smith).

"Title Registration and Land Reform: A Reply," 8 *University of Chicago Law Review* 63 (1940).

"Argument in Favor of the Constitutionality of the Pepper Bill," 21 *Congressional Digest* 272 (1942).

"Future Interests Restated: Tradition versus Clarification and Reform," 55 *Harvard Law Review* 1077 (1942).

"Public Purpose in Public Housing: An Anachronism Reburied," 52 *Yale Law Journal* 42 (1942) (with Addison A. Mueller).

"Legal Education and Public Policy: Professional Training in the Public Interest," 52 *Yale Law Journal* 203 (1943) (with Harold D. Lasswell); *reprinted in* McDougal & Associates, *Studies in World Public Order* 42 (1960), and H. Lasswell, *The Analysis of Political Behavior: An Empirical Approach* 21 (1948).

"Policy-making as the Center of Emphasis," *Handbook, Association of American Law Schools* 47 (1943).

"Aims and Objectives of Legal Education," *Handbook, Association of American Law Schools* 125 (1945).

"Treaties and Congressional-Executive or Presidential Agreements: Interchangeable Instruments of National Policy," 54 *Yale Law Journal* 181, 534 (1945) (with Asher Lans); *reprinted in* McDougal & Associates, *Studies in World Public Order* 404 (1960).

"Municipal Land Policy and Control," 242 *Annals of the American Academy of Political and Social Science* 88 (1945).

"A Regional Development Administration," 4 *New England War Bulletin* 14 (June–July 1945).

"The Law School of the Future: From Legal Realism to Policy Science in the World Community," 56 *Yale Law Journal* 1345 (1947).

"The Codification of International Law," 41 *Proceedings, American Soc'y of International Law* 47 (1947).

"Regional Planning and Development: The Process of Using Intelligence Under Conditions of Resource and Institutional Interdependency, for Securing Community Values," 32 *Iowa Law Review* 193 (1947).

"The Role of Law in World Politics," 20 *Mississippi Law Journal* 253 (1949).

"The Rights of Man in World Community: Constitutional Illusional Versus Rational Action," 14 *Law and Contemporary Problems* 90 (1949); 59 *Yale Law Journal* 60 (1949); *reprinted in* McDougal & Associates, *Studies in World Public Order* 335 (1960).

"The Genocide Convention and the Constitution," 3 *Vanderbilt Law Review* 683 (1950) (with Richard Arens).

"Planning and Development for Metropolitan Communities," 1950 *American Planning and Civic Annual* 94 (1950).

"The Veto and the Charter: An Interpretation for Survival," 60 *Yale Law Journal* 258 (1951) (with Richard N. Gardner), *reprinted in* McDougal & Associates, *Studies in World Public Order* 718 (1960).

"The Comparative Study of Law for Policy Purposes: Value Clarification as an Instrument of Democratic World Order," 1 *American Journal of Comparative Law* 24 (1952); *reprinted in* 61 *Yale Law Journal* 915 (1952); *reprinted in* McDougal & Associates, *Studies in World Public Order* 947 (1960).

"Law and Power." 46 *American Journal of International Law* 102 (1952), *reprinted in International Law in the Twentieth Century* 104 (L. Gross, ed.) (1969).

"The Treaty-making Power," *Proceedings of the International Law Association* (American Branch) 13 (1952).

Vita & Bibliography

"Dr. Schwarzenberger's Power Politics," 47 *American Journal of International Law* 115 (1953) (a review of G. Schwarzenberger, *Power Politics: A Study of International Society* (2d rev. ed., 1951)).

"International Law, Power and Policy: A Contemporary Conception," 82 *Recueil des Cours* 133 (1953).

"The Treaty Power and the Constitution: The Case Against the [Bricker] Amendment," 40 *American Bar Association Journal* 203 (1954) (with Brunson MacChesney and others).

"The Policy Science Approach to International Legal Studies," in *International Law and the United Nations,* Eighth Summer Institute, University of Michigan Law School, 1955.

"The Influence of the Metropolis on Concepts, Rules and Institutions Relating to Property," 4 *Journal of Public Law* 93 (1955); *reprinted in* abridged form as "The Impact of the Metropolis Upon Land Law," *The Metropolis in Modern Life* 212 (R. Fisher, ed. 1955).

"The Realist Theory in Pyrrhic Victory, 49 *American Journal of International Law* 376 (1955) (a review of H. Morgenthau, *Politics Among Nations* (2d ed., 1954)).

"The Hydrogen Bomb Tests in Perspective: Lawful Measures for Security," 64 *Yale Law Journal* 648 (1955) (with Norbert A. Schlei), *reprinted in* McDougal & Associates, *Studies in World Public Order* 763 (1960).

"The Hydrogen Bomb Tests and the International Law of the Sea," 49 *American Journal of International Law* 356 (1955).

"Peace and War: Factual Continuum with Multiple Legal Consequences," 49 *American Journal of International Law* 63 (1955).

"Law as a Process of Decision: A Policy-oriented Approach to Legal Study," 1 *Natural Law Forum* 53 (1956).

"El Derecho Internacional Como Ciencia Politica," 3 *Revista de Derecho y Ciencias Sociales* 142 (1956).

"Jurisdiction," 9 *Naval War College Review* 1 (1957).

"Artificial Satellites: A Modest Proposal," 51 *American Journal of International Law* 74 (1957).

"Crisis in the Law of the Sea: Community Perspectives versus National Egoism," 67 *Yale Law Journal* 539 (1958) (with William T. Burke); *reprinted in* McDougal & Burke, *The Public Order of the Oceans* 1 (1962).

"The Initiation of Coercion: A Multitemporal Analysis," 52 *American Journal of International Law* 241 (1958) (with Florentino P. Feliciano); *reprinted in* McDougal & Feliciano, *Law and Minimum World Public Order: The Legal Regulation of International Coercion* 97 (1961).

"International Coercion and World Public Order: The General Principles of the Law of War," 67 *Yale Law Journal* 771 (1958) (with Florentino P. Feliciano); *reprinted in* McDougal & Feliciano, *Law and Minimum World Public Order: The Legal Regulation of International Coercion* 1 (1961) and McDougal & Associates, *Studies in World Public Order* 237 (1960).

"Perspectives for a Law of Outer Space," 52 *American Journal of International Law* 407 (1958) (with Leon S. Lipson); *reprinted in* McDougal & Associates, *Studies in World Public Order* 912 (1960).

"The Identification and Appraisal of Diverse Systems of Public Order," 53 *American Journal of International Law* 1 (1959); *reprinted in* McDougal & Associates, *Studies in World Public Order* 3 (1960); *reprinted in International Law in the Twentieth Century* 169 (L. Gross, ed.) (1969).

"International Law and Contending World Orders," *Proceedings of the 1958 Institute of World Affairs* 11 (1959).

"Legal Regulation of Resort to International Coercion: Aggression and Self-Defense in Policy Perspective," 68 *Yale Law Journal* 1057 (1959) (with Florentino P. Feliciano); *reprinted in* McDougal & Feliciano, *Law and Minimum World Public Order: The Legal Regulation of International Coercion* 121 (1961).

"The Impact of International Law Upon National Law: A Policy-oriented Perspective," 4 *South Dakota Law Review* 25 (1959); *reprinted in* McDougal & Associates, *Studies in World Public Order* 157 (1960).

"Perspectives for an International Law of Human Dignity," 53 *Proceedings of the American Society of International Law* 107 (1959); *reprinted in* McDougal & Associates, *Studies in World Public Order* 987 (1960).

"The Community Interest in a Narrow Territorial Sea: Inclusive versus Exclusive Competence over the Oceans," 45 *Cornell Law Quarterly* 171 (1960) (with William T. Burke); *reprinted in* McDougal & Burke, *The Public Order of the Oceans* 446 (1962).

"Community Prohibitions of International Coercion and Sanctioning Processes: The Technique of World Public Order," 35 *Philippine Law Journal* 1256 (1960) (with

Florentino P. Feliciano); *reprinted in* McDougal & Feliciano, *Law and Minimum World Public Order: The Legal Regulation of International Coercion* 261, 383 (1961).

"Some Basic Theoretical Concepts about International Law: A Policy-oriented Framework of Inquiry," 4 *Journal of Conflict Resolution* 337 (1960); *reprinted in, The Strategy of World Order* vol. 2, 116 (R. Falk and S. Mendlowitz, eds.) (1966).

"The Maintenance of Public Order at Sea and the Nationality of Ships, 54 *American Journal of International Law* 25 (1960) (with William T. Burke and Ivan A. Vlasic); *reprinted in* McDougal & Burke, *The Public Order of the Oceans* 1008 (1962).

"The Ethics of Applying Systems of Authority: The Balanced Opposites of a Legal System," *in The Ethics of Power* 221 (H. Lasswell and H. Cleveland, eds.) (1962).

"Claims to Authority Over the Territorial Sea," 1 *Philippine International Law Journal* 29 (1962) (with William T. Burke).

"The Soviet-Cuban Quarantine and Self-Defense," 57 *American Journal of International Law* 597 (1963); *reprinted in International Law in the Twentieth Century* 716 (L. Gross, ed.) (1969).

"Fundamental Challenges to Legal Doctrines Affecting International Coercion: Aggression, Self-Defense, Non-intervention, Self-Determination, Neutrality," (Panel discussion) 57 *Proceedings of the American Society of International Law* 163 (1963).

"Emerging Customary Law of Space," 58 *Northwestern University Law Review* 618 (1963).

"Enjoyment and Acquisition of Resources in Outer Space," 111 *University of Pennsylvania Law Review* 521 (1963) (with Harold D. Lasswell, Ivan A. Vlasic & Joseph Smith); *reprinted in* McDougal, et al., *Law and Public Order in Space* 749 (1963).

"Law and Public Order in Space," *in Proceedings on Space Science and Space Law* 151 (M. Schwartz, ed. 1963).

"Foreword," *in* W. Weyrauch, *The Personality of Lawyers* xi (with Harold D. Lasswell) (1964).

"Human Rights in the United Nations," 58 *American Journal of International Law* 603 (1964) (with Gerhard Bebr).

"Foreword: Sanctions in Context," 49 *Iowa Law Review* 229 (1964).

"Enforcing International Law Against one Country Through Domestic Litigation in Others," (Panel discussion) 58 *Proceedings of the American Society of International Law* 33, 48 (1964) (with W. Reese, J. Laylin & E. Re).

"The Prospects for a Regime in Outer Space," *in* M. Cohen, *Law and Politics in Space* 105 (1964).

Brief amicus curiae of the Executive Committee of the International Law Association (American Branch) *Banco Nacional de Cuba v. Sabbatino* 376, U.S. 398 (1964) (of counsel with P. Kooiman & C. Olmstead).

"The Changing Structure of International Law: Unchanging Theory for Inquiry," 65 *Columbia Law Review* 810 (1965) (with W. Michael Reisman).

Testimony on the Sabbatino Amendment, *in* U.S. Congress, House, Committee on Foreign Affairs, Hearings on H.R. 7750, 89th Congress, 1st Session, 1033 (1965).

"Chinese Participation in the United Nations: The Legal Imperatives of A Negotiated Solution," 60 *American Journal of International Law* (October, 1966) (with R. Goodman).

"Act of State in Policy Perspective: The International Law of an International Economy," *in Private Investors Abroad—Structures and Safeguards* 327 (V. Cameron ed., 1966) (Chapter in Annual Volume, *The Southwestern Legal Foundation,* 1966–67).

"Jurisprudence For a Free Society," 1 *Georgia Law Review* 1 (Fall 1966).

Letter to President Lyndon Johnson (Feb. 14, 1966) in reply to the Lawyers' Committee on American Policy toward Vietnam, 112 *Congressional Record* 3842 (Feb. 26, 1966).

"Legal Education for a Free Society: Our Collective Responsibility" (Presidential Address), *Association of American Law Schools, Proceedings,* Part Two, 33 (December 1966); *reprinted in Politics, Personality and Social Science in the Twentieth Century: Essays in Honor of Harold D. Lasswell* 383 (A. Rogow, ed.) (1969).

"Education for Professional Responsibility," 12(1) *The Student Lawyer* 6 (October 1966).

"The Role of the Law School in Continuing Legal Education—Part II," 13(6) *Practical Lawyer* 6 (1967) (with W. E. Sell, R. Malone, P. Coogan, F. Stumpf & H. Wechsler).

"The International Law Commission's Draft Articles Upon Interpretation: Textuality Redivivus," 61 *American Journal of International Law* 992 (October 1967).

"Authority to Use Force on the High Seas," 20 *Naval War College Review* 19 (1967).

"Jurisprudence in Policy Oriented Perspective," XIX:3 *University of Florida Law Review* 486–513 (1967) (with Harold D. Lasswell).

"International Law and the Law of the Sea" *in The Law of the Sea: Offshore Boundaries and Zones* 3 (Lewis M. Alexander, ed.) (Ohio State University Press, 1967).

Statement Upon National Foundation for Social Sciences, Hearings Before Subcommittee on Government Research of the Committee on Government Operations, U.S. Senate 90th Congress, 1st Session, on S. 836, pp.508–551 (U.S. Gov't. Printing Office, 1967).

"Jurisprudence in Policy-oriented Perspective," 19 *University of Florida Law Review* 486 (1967) (with Harold Lasswell).

"The World Constitutive Process of Authoritative Decision," 19 *Journal of Legal Education* 253, 403 (1967) (with Harold D. Lasswell and W. Michael Reisman), *reprinted in The Future of the International Legal Order* vol. 1, 73 (C. Black & R. Falk, eds. 1969) and in McDougal & Reisman, *International Law Essays* 191 (1981).

"Authority to Use Force on the High Seas," 20 *Naval War College Review* 19 (December 1967).

Statement to the Committee of the Whole on the "Vienna Conference on the Law of Treaties," April 19, 1968, 62 *American Journal of International Law* 1021 (1968).

"Reflections of a Fellow Teacher," 17 *Catholic University Law Review* 291 (1968).

"Rhodesia and the United Nations: The Lawfulness of International Concern," 62 *American Journal of International Law* 1 (January 1968) (with W. Michael Reisman); *reprinted in* slightly different form as "A Reply to Dean Acheson," 2 *International Lawyer* 729 (1968).

"Theories About International Law: Prologue to a Configurative Jurisprudence," 8 *Virginia Journal of International Law* 188 (April 1968) (with Harold D. Lasswell & W. Michael Reisman).

"In Dedication to Dean Dillard: Man of Depth and Style," 54 *Virginia Law Review* 585 (May 1968) (with Harold D. Lasswell).

"Revision of the Geneva Conventions on the Law of the Sea—The Views of a Commentator," 1:3 *Natural Resources Lawyer* 19 (July 1968).

"Statement Upon Interpretation, The Vienna Conference on the Law of Treaties," 2 *American Journal of International Law,* 1021–1027, (October 1968).

"Theories About International Law: Prologue to a Configurative Jurisprudence," 8:2 *Virginia Journal of International Law* 189 (1968) (with Harold D. Lasswell and W. Michael Reisman), *reprinted in* McDougal & Reisman, *International Law Essays* 43 (1981).

"Foreword," *in* R. Hull & J. Novogrod, *Law and Vietnam* vii (1968).

"Foreword," *in* John N. Moore, *Law and the Indo-China War* vii (1972).

"Human Rights and World Public Order: A Framework for Policy-oriented Inquiry," 63 *American Journal of International Law* 237 (April 1969) (with Harold D. Lasswell & Lung-chu Chen).

"Third Party Decision," 63 *American Journal of International Law* 685 (1969).

"The World Constitutive Process of Authoritative Decision," *in The Future of the International Legal Order,* vol. 1 (C. Black & R. Falk, eds.) (Princeton University Press, 1969) (with Harold D. Lasswell and W. Michael Reisman).

Commentary upon "Prospects for Agreement, The Law of the Sea: A New Geneva Conference," *Proceedings of the Sixth Conference of the Law of the Sea Institute,* University of Rhode Island, 50, 68, 118, 179, 201 (1971).

"Legal Bases for Securing the Integrity of the Earth-Space Environment," 184 *Annals of the New York Academy of Sciences* 375 (1971); *reprinted in Multitudo legum ius unum: Festschrift für Wilhelm Wengler zu seinem* vol. 1, 261 (1973); *reprinted* with minor changes in 8:2 *Journal of Natural Resources & Environmental Law* 177 (1994).

"Criteria for a Theory About Law," 44:2 *Southern California Law Review* 362 (1971) (with Harold D. Lasswell).

"International Law and Social Science: A Mild Plea in Avoidance," 66 *American Journal of International Law* 77 (1972).

"Trends in Theories about Law: Comprehensiveness in Conceptions of Constitutive Process," 41 *George Washington Law Review* 1 (1972) (with Harold D. Lasswell).

"The Teaching of International Law," 2 *Georgia Journal of International & Comparative Law* 111 (1972, Supp. 2).

Letter to Senator Barry Goldwater (Jan. 12, 1973), *in* "Goldwater, The President's Constitutional Primacy in Foreign Relations and National Defense," 13 *Virginia Journal of International Law* 472 (1973).

"The Objectives of Professional Training in Community Interest," *in* S. K. Agrawala, *Legal Education in India: Problems and Perspectives* 62 (1973).

"The Intelligence Function and World Public Order," 46 *Temple Law Quarterly* 365 (1973).

"The Law of the High Seas in Time of Peace," 25 *Naval War College Review* 35 (1973); *also in* 3 *Denver Journal of International Law and Policy* 45 (1973).

"The Protection of the Environment and World Public Order: Some Recent Developments," 45 *Mississippi Law Journal* 1085 (1974) (with Jan Schneider).

"Nationality and Human Rights: The Protection of the Individual in External Arenas," 83 *Yale Law Journal* 900 (1974).

"Human Rights and World Public Order: Principles of Content and Procedure for Clarifying General Community Policies," 14 *Virginia Journal of International Law* 387 (1974).

"Beware of the Squid Function," 1 *Learning & the Law* 16 (Spring 1974).

"Human Rights for Women and World Public Order: The Outlawing of Sex-based Discrimination," 69 *American Journal of International Law* 497 (1975) (with Harold D. Lasswell & Lung-chu Chen).

"The Protection of Respect and Human Rights: Freedom of Choice and World Public Order," 24 *American University Law Review* 919 (1975) (with Harold D. Lasswell & Lung-chu Chen).

"Relation of Law to Social Process: Trends in Theories about Law," 37 *University of Pittsburgh Law Review* 465 (with Harold Lasswell) (1976).

"Freedom from Discrimination in Choice of Language and International Human Rights," 1976 *Southern Illinois University Law Journal* 151 (1976) (with Harold D. Lasswell & Lung-chu Chen).

"Trends in Theories about Law: Maintaining Observational Standpoint and Delimiting the Focus of Inquiry," 8 *University of Toledo Law Review* 1 (with Harold Lasswell) (1976).

"Human Rights of the Aged: An Application of the General Norm of Nondiscrimination," 28 *University of Florida Law Review* 639 (1976) (with Harold D. Lasswell & Lung-chu Chen).

"Protection of Aliens from Discrimination and World Public Order: Responsibility of States Conjoined with Human Rights," 70 *American Journal of International Law* 432 (1976) (with Harold D. Lasswell & Lung-chu Chen).

"Right to Religious Freedom and World Public Order: The Emerging Norm of Nondiscrimination," 74 *Michigan Law Review* 865 (1976) (with Harold D. Lasswell & Lung-chu Chen).

"Aggregate Interest in Shared Respect and Human Rights: The Harmonization of Public Order and Civic Order," 23 *New York Law School Law Review* 183 (1977) (with Harold D. Lasswell & Lung-chu Chen).

Myres Smith McDougal

"Human Rights and World Public Order: Human Rights in Comprehensive Context," 72 *Northwestern University Law Review* 227 (1977) (with Harold D. Lasswell & Lung-chu Chen).

"The Application of Constitutive Prescriptions: An Addendum to Justice Cardozo." Thirty-Third Annual Benjamin N. Cardozo Lecture Delivered Before the Association of the Bar of the City of New York, October 13, 1977; *reprinted in 33 Record of the Association of the Bar of the City of New York* 255 (1978).

"Harold Dwight Lasswell, 1902–1978," 73 *American Journal of International Law* 655 (1979) (with W. Michael Reisman).

"Harold Dwight Lasswell, 1902–1978," 88 *Yale Law Journal* 675 (1979).

"The World Community: A Planetary Social Process," 21:3 *U.C. Davis Law Review* 807 (1988) (with W. Michael Reisman & Andrew R. Willard).

"The Dorsey Comment: A Modest Retrogression," 82 *American Journal of International Law* 51 (Jan. 1988).

"The World Process of Effective Power: The Global War System," *in Power and Policy in Quest of Law* (M. McDougal & W. M. Reisman eds.) (Dordrecht, The Netherlands: Martinus Nijhoff Publishers, 1985) (with W. Michael Reisman & Andrew R. Willard).

"The World Community: A Planetary Social Process," 21 *University of California at Davis Law Review* 807 (Spring, 1988) (with W. Michael Reisman & Andrew R. Willard).

"Law and Peace," 18:1 *Denver Journal of International Law and Policy* 1 (Fall 1989).

"International Law in Policy-Oriented Perspective," *in The Structure and Process of International Law* (abridged edition) (R. St. J. Macdonald & D.M. Johnston, eds., 1989) (with W. Michael Reisman).

"Law and Peace in a Changing World," 22 *Cumberland Law Review* 681 (1991/92) (with Siegfried Wiessner).

Remarks of Myres S. McDougal (in connection with Lifetime Achievement Award) 66 *Mississippi Law Journal* 15 (1996).

BOOK REVIEWS

Review of Tooke, *Cases on the Law of Municipal Corporations* (1931), 27 *Illinois Law Review* 469 (1932).

Review of Everett, *The Education of Jeremy Bentham* (1931), 27 *Illinois Law Review* 580 (1933).

Review of Walsh, *A Treatise on Mortgages* (1934), 44 *Yale Law Journal* 1278 (1935).

Review of Hanna, *Cases and Materials on Creditors' Rights*, (2d ed. 1935), 45 *Yale Law Journal* 1159 (1936).

Review of Holbrook & Aigler, *Cases on the Law of Bankruptcy*, (T.C. Billig, ed.) (3d ed. 1936), 45 *Yale Law Journal* 1158 (1936).

Review of American Law Institute, 1–2 *Restatement of the Law of Property* (1936), 32 *Illinois Law Review* 508 (1937).

Review of Hutchins, *The Higher Learning in America* (1936), 46 *Yale Law Journal* 1433 (1937).

Review of Smith, *The Promise of American Politics* (1936), 46 *Yale Law Journal* 1269 (1937).

Review of Brown, *A Treatise on the Law of Personal Property* (1936), 47 *Yale Law Journal* 514 (1938).

Review of Chase, *The Tyranny of Words* (1938), 5 *University of Chicago Law Review* 702 (1938).

Review of Hall, *Readings in Jurisprudence* (1938), 34 *Illinois Law Review* 109 (1939).

Review of Radin, *The Law and Mr. Smith* (1938), 87 *University of Pennsylvania Law Review* 495 (1939).

Review of American Law Institute, 4 *Restatement of the Law of Torts*, Ch. 41 (on "natural rights" of property holders) (1939), 49 *Yale Law Journal* 1502 (1940) (with Charles Runyon).

Review of Ebenstein, *The Law of Public Housing* (1940), 54 *Harvard Law Review* 526 (1941).

Review of Fuller, *The Law in Quest of Itself* (Fuller vs. the American Legal Realists: An Intervention) (1941), 50 *Yale Law Journal* 827 (1941).

Review of Clark, *Real Covenants and Other Interests which "Run with the Land"* (1947), 58 *Yale Law Journal* 500 (1949).

Review of Lauterpacht, *International Law and Human Rights* (1950), 60 *Yale Law Journal* 1051 (1951).

Review of Simpson & Stone, *Cases and Readings on Law and Society*, (1948–49), 45 *American Journal of International Law* 399 (1951).

Review of Lissitsyn, *The International Court of Justice* (1951), 47 *American Journal of International Law* 340 (1953).

Review of Bryson et al., *Foundations of World Organization* (1952), 47 *American Journal of International Law* 351 (1953).

Review of Konvitz, *Civil Rights in Immigration* (1953), 48 *American Journal of International Law* 335 (1954).

Review of Stern, *The Struggle for Poland* (1953), 48 *American Journal of International Law* 525 (1954).

Review of Wright, *Problems of Stability and Progress in International Relations* (1954), 48 *American Journal of International Law* 680 (1954).

Review of Swarztrauber, *The Three Mile Limit of Territorial Seas* (1972), 7 *International Lawyer* 925 (1973).

Edited by Cheryl A. DeFilippo,
W. Michael Reisman,
Elizabeth Stauderman, and Andrew R. Willard

Produced by the Office of Public Affairs,
Yale Law School

————————

2,000 copies were printed at Herlin Press
and bound by Mueller Trade Bindery
with production supervision by
Yale Reprographic & Imaging Services

This book is set in the Dante types
Design & typography by Howard I. Gralla